MW00561762

Weekend Word

A One-Year Devotional

Capresha Caldwell

Scripture quotations marked (NIV) are taken from the Holy Bible, New International Version®, NIV®. Copyright © 1973, 1978, 1984, 2011 by Biblica, Inc.® Used by permission of Zondervan. All rights reserved worldwide. www.zondervan.com The "NIV" and "New International Version" are trademarks registered in the United States Patent and Trademark Office by Biblica, Inc.®

Scripture quotations marked MSG are taken from THE MESSAGE, copyright © 1993, 2002, 2018 by Eugene H. Peterson. Used by permission of NavPress, represented by Tyndale House Publishers. All rights reserved.

Scripture quotations marked (AMP) are taken from the Amplified Bible, Copyright © 1954, 1958, 1962, 1964, 1965, 1987 by The Lockman Foundation. Used by permission.

Scripture quotations marked (NKJV) are taken from the New King James Version®. Copyright © 1982 by Thomas Nelson. Used by permission. All rights reserved.

Scripture quotations marked (ERV) are taken from the Holy Bible: Easy-to-Read Version (ERV), International Edition © 2013, 2016 by Bible League International and used by permission.

Scripture quotations marked (GNT) are from the Good News Translation in Today's English Version- Second Edition Copyright © 1992 by American Bible Society. Used by Permission.

Scripture quotations marked (AMPC) are taken from the Amplified® Bible (AMPC), Copyright © 1954, 1958, 1962, 1964, 1965, 1987 by The Lockman Foundation used by permission. www.lockman.org

Scripture quotations marked (TLB) are taken from The Living Bible copyright © 1971. Used by permission of Tyndale House Publishers, Carol Stream, Illinois 60188. All rights reserved.

Dedication

I dedicate this book to the women in my family.
Thank you each for your love and support.

Table of Contents

Weekend 1

Dear friend, I pray that you may enjoy good health and that all may go well with you, even as your soul is getting along well.
3 John 1:2 (NIV)

Beloved, I pray that you may prosper in all things and be in heath, just as your soul prospers.
3 John 1:2 (NKJV)

I started Whole Woman several years ago to help women experience being complete in the Lord. This Outreach continues to evolve and is built on 3 John 1:2. I have experienced God's love and healing power, which has absolutely changed and improved my life. God has filled and continues to fill every area of my life to overflow. He is so faithful and I'm ecstatic to share this platform this year with other awesome women of God. They will provide great insight and ministry about the awesomeness of God!

Expect to see the blessings of the Lord in every aspect of your life. Prayerfully set goals for your life and ask God for wisdom to create a strategy. Overcome fear and choose to try something new! Have the right attitude and connect with the right people. Enjoy life on purpose! Laugh more this year than in previous years. Stop doing the same thing and expecting a different result! Remember God wants you to have a blessed life, so go for it!

IN FAITH MOVE FORWARD!

PEACE

Friday

Date: _____

You will keep *him* in perfect peace, *Whose* mind *is* stayed *on You,* Because he trusts in You. **-Isaiah 26:3 (NKJV) (emphasized added)**

Make a decision to stay focused on and trust in God. In the midst of any situation, you can have peace. Your peace does not depend on circumstances. Life will change but God is consistent and can always keep you in peace.

Personal Reflection and Application:

_____

_____

_____

_____

_____

_____

_____

_____

_____

_____

_____

_____

_____

_____

LOVE

Saturday

Date: _____

He who does not love does not know God, for God is love. **-1 John 4:8 (NKJV)**

Remember—God IS love! These three words and the overall scripture gives us great insight about God *Himself*. He IS love. Love is the very core of who God is, and His character does not change. Since He is love, He loves you and everything that He does towards you and for you is motivated by love.

Personal Reflection and Application:

_____

_____

_____

_____

_____

_____

_____

_____

_____

_____

_____

_____

_____

_____

GRACE

Sunday

Date: _____

For it is by grace [God's remarkable compassion and favor drawing you to Christ] that you have been saved [actually delivered from judgment and given eternal life] through faith. And this [salvation] is not of yourselves [not through your own effort], but it is the [undeserved, gracious] gift of God; [9] not as a result of [your] works [nor your attempts to keep the Law], so that no one will [be able to] boast *or* take credit in any way [for his salvation]. **Ephesians 2:8-9(AMP)**

Can you comprehend God's grace? It is truly mind blowing. In the Amplified translation above, grace is explained as God's unmerited favor. Unmerited means something that is 'undeserved.' We don't 'deserve' it … Salvation is a GIFT from God.

Personal Reflection and Application:

_____

_____

_____

_____

_____

_____

_____

_____

_____

_____

_____

Weekend 2

And suddenly, a woman who had a flow of blood for twelve years came from behind and touched the hem of His garment. For she said to herself, "If I only touch His garment, I shall be made well." But Jesus turned around, and when He saw her He said, "Be of good cheer, daughter; your faith has made you well." And the woman was made well from that hour. -**Matthew 9:20-23 (NKJV)**

I was listening to a sermon one day and he referenced this scripture. I heard this scripture many times before but received new revelation. He said that this woman put a demand on the supply. In other words, Jesus has the ability and authority to heal her, so He had the 'supply'. She built up her faith and that was the demand. Honestly, that's how I feel right now. There are things that I have been dealing with for decades and enough is enough! I am putting a demand on the supply. I am getting radical! I need to press into His presence and build my faith. I'm listening to the Word more at work and home. She received her healing in that very hour. No more delay! I am receiving my deliverance and healing this very hour. Receive your deliverance and healing!

LIFE

Friday

Date: _____

I shall not die, but live, And declare the works of the LORD. **-Psalm 118:17 (NKJV)**

Don't allow anything to hinder your progress, discourage you or bring you down. You have encountered previous disappointments, frustrations and maybe any failures but you still have opportunities and hope. Make a decision to live out loud and go forth boldly in what God has called you to do. Your courageous actions of fulfilling God's purpose for your life speaks volumes of His goodness. You are alive, so live!

Personal Reflection and Application:

_____
_____
_____
_____
_____
_____
_____
_____
_____
_____
_____
_____
_____

RESTORATION

Saturday

Date: _____

Then the Lord God said to the woman, "What is this you have done?" The woman said, "The serpent deceived me, and I ate." **-Genesis 3:13 (NIV)**

This week I was reflecting on some areas of my life and started wondering if I made a mistake and messed up some things that God had planned. Then I saw a post from a Facebook friend that said "If you think you've blown God's plan for your life, rest in this. You, my friend, are not that powerful." That message really encouraged my heart! Yes, Eve was deceived by the serpent and made a mistake and then Adam made the same mistake, and they were kicked out of the Garden of Eden. However, God already had a plan of restoration thru Christ Jesus. For your shortcomings and mistakes, God already has a plan to restore you!

Personal Reflection and Application:

_____
_____
_____
_____
_____
_____
_____
_____
_____
_____
_____
_____
_____
_____

VICTORY

Sunday

Date: _____

And he said, "Listen, all you of Judah and you inhabitants of Jerusalem, and you, King Jehoshaphat! Thus, says the Lord to you: 'Do not be afraid nor dismayed because of this great multitude, for the battle *is* not yours, but God's. Tomorrow go down against them. They will surely come up by the Ascent of Ziz, and you will find them at the end of the brook before the Wilderness of Jeruel. You will not *need* to fight in this *battle*. Position yourselves, stand still and see the salvation of the Lord, who is with you, O Judah and Jerusalem!' Do not fear or be dismayed; tomorrow go out against them, for the Lord *is* with you. **-2 Chronicles 20:15-17 (NKJV)(emphasis added)**

Jehoshaphat knew he could not win the battle alone. He put his faith in God! You are not facing your 'battles' alone. Trust God for the Victory!

Personal Reflection and Application:

_____
_____
_____
_____
_____
_____
_____
_____
_____
_____
_____
_____

Weekend 3

"There is no fear in love; but perfect love casts out fear, because fear involves torment. But he who fears has not been made perfect in love." -1 John 4:18 (NKJV)

I was walking through a parking lot in Uptown Charlotte one day when I heard footsteps behind me. My heart started racing and as the footsteps began to run (getting closer) I screamed and started running. I turned around and saw two children (one was a toddler and the other, a little older) running with their mother to their car. I stopped dead in my tracks and laughed at how silly I must have looked. Fear, especially of the unknown, can cause us to have irrational thoughts (I really thought someone was about to try to harm me- in the middle of this parking lot, with multiple people around, in the middle if the day). We can end up looking silly because we are afraid of things that are not real or not as big or scary as we think they are (after all, I was running from children). Truth be told, all I had to do was turn around when I heard the footsteps, and I would have seen there was nothing to fear. But instead of assessing the situation so I could make a sound decision, I allowed fear to control my actions. As Christians we have nothing to fear. God loves, covers, and protects us. John tells us that "there is no fear in love: but perfect love (God's love) casteth out fear: because fear hath torment." There is no peace in fear, but peace can be found by accepting God's love. Make a choice to accept God's love, to rest in His peace, and to not allow fear to control you.

Contributor- Bry-Anne E. Jones, MSW, LCSW

ARMOR OF GOD

Friday

Date: _____

Put on the whole armor of God, that you may be able to stand against the wiles of the devil. For we do not wrestle against flesh and blood, but against principalities, against powers, against the rulers of the darkness of this age, against spiritual *hosts* of wickedness in the heavenly *places.* Therefore, *take up* the whole armor of God, that you may be able to withstand in the evil day, and having done all, to stand. **-Ephesians 6:11 – 13 (NKJV)**

I highlighted a portion of the texts in verses 11 and 13. One thing my Pastor says is if something is repeated in the Bible pay close attention. In these scriptures, we are instructed twice that we need to put on the Armor of God. Have you ever given instructions to someone and repeated yourself to emphasize the importance? Same thing here – it's important for you to act daily and put on His armor!

Personal Reflection and Application:

_____
_____
_____
_____
_____
_____
_____
_____
_____
_____

ROOTED IN LOVE

Saturday

Date: _____

For this reason I bow my knees to the Father of our Lord Jesus Christ, from whom the whole family in heaven and earth is named, that He would grant you, according to the riches of His glory, to be strengthened with might through His Spirit in the inner man, that Christ may dwell in your hearts through faith; that you, being rooted and grounded in love, may be able to comprehend with all the saints what is the width and length and depth and height— to know the love of Christ which passes knowledge; that you may be filled with all the fullness of God. Ephesians **3:14–19 (NKJV)**

GOD IS LOVE (1 John 4:8). When you are rooted and grounded in love, you are actually rooted and grounded in God. Stay in faith and trust God. Your root system is secure and in good ground, so you can withstand anything!

Personal Reflection and Application:

_____
_____
_____
_____
_____
_____
_____
_____
_____
_____
_____

VICTORY IN JESUS

Sunday

Date: _____

But thanks be to God, who gives us the victory through our Lord Jesus Christ. **-1 Corinthians 15:57 (NKJV)**

Lift your hands and voice to give God praise! Now tell that challenging situation, "I have the victory through Christ! Finances, health, relationship, _____ (fill in the blank). I have the victory through Christ! Glory to God!"

Personal Reflection and Application:

_____
_____
_____
_____
_____
_____
_____
_____
_____
_____
_____

Weekend 4

Now to him who is able to do immeasurably more than all we ask or imagine, according to his power that is at work within us.
-Ephesians 3:20 (NIV)

My toddler was upstairs and came running around the corner screaming daddy because she heard his truck coming into the neighborhood. By the time my husband parked the truck, she was downstairs waiting by the door. Some of the older kids still do this. Maybe the thought is their daddy is bringing them something... or relationship compelled them. But there is an expectation of the father. We can think the same when it comes to our Heavenly Father. You can have an expectation of Him, and He should have an expectation of you. Why? Because expectation is a two-way street.
My husband cannot be in a healthy committed relationship with me without expectation and vice versa. God should expect us to be people who love Him and his people, faithful, keeper of his commandments. Decide today to increase your expectation of God and in return increase your anticipation of what God can do.

Contributor- Roshanda "The Rosho" Pratt, First Lady of Visibility

PEACE

Friday

Date: _____

Finally, brethren, whatever things are true, whatever things are noble, whatever things are just, whatever things are pure, whatever things are lovely, whatever things are of good report, if there is any virtue and if there is anything praiseworthy—meditate on these things. The things which you learned and received and heard and saw in me, these do, and the God of peace will be with you. **Philippians 4:8-9 (NKJV)**

Have you ever imagined a sad situation and then tears came to your eyes? Your thought life is powerful, and you can control your thoughts! When a seemingly random thought comes to mind, determine whether it is the right one to meditate on because it impacts your well-being! As I have heard a popular Christian teacher say, think about what you are thinking about.

Personal Reflection and Application:

_____
_____
_____
_____
_____
_____
_____
_____
_____
_____
_____
_____

HOPE

Saturday

Date: _____

These two things cannot change: God cannot lie when he says something, and he cannot lie when he makes an oath. So these two things are a great help to us who have come to God for safety. They encourage us to hold on to the hope that is ours. This hope is like an anchor for us. It is strong and sure and keeps us safe. It goes behind the curtain. **-Hebrews 6:18-19 (ERV)**

When you have hope, you have an expectation for something good to happen! Hope is the anchor for your soul! Your soul includes your mind, will, and emotions. Hopelessness can cause feelings of sadness and depression. An anchor holds a ship in position despite the winds and the rains. In order to weather the storms of life, you must put your hope in God!

Personal Reflection and Application:

_____
_____
_____
_____
_____
_____
_____
_____
_____
_____
_____

LOVE

Sunday

Date: _____

In this the love of God was manifested toward us, that God has sent His only begotten Son into the world, that we might live through Him. **-1 John 4:9 (NKJV)**

As the old saying goes - actions speak louder than words! If you ever wonder about God's love, look at His actions. He sent Christ to give you a blessed life here on earth and eternal life with Him. Your circumstances, situations, and experiences don't change the fact that God loves YOU!

Personal Reflection and Application:

_____

_____

_____

_____

_____

_____

_____

_____

_____

Weekend 5

Success

This book of the law shall not depart out of <u>your</u> mouth; but <u>you</u> shall read it [mediate on] it day and night, so that <u>you</u> may be careful to do [everything] in accordance with all that is written in it; for then <u>you</u> will make <u>your</u> way prosperous, and then <u>you</u> will be successful." **-Joshua 1:8 (AMP)(emphasize added)**

For most of my life I discredited myself due to fear, lack of resources and motivation? God said that I can be prosperous and successful if I am faithful to His word. My ability to be effective has nothing to do with others and everything to do with me. The gifts, talents and abilities that God has invested in me became active when I studied His word and applied it. Success requires that I MOVE!

Contributor- Shanita L. Rogers, Author, Public Speaker & Moderator

RELY ON HOLY SPIRIT

Friday

Date: _____

However, when He, the Spirit of truth, has come, He will guide you into all truth; for He will not speak on His own authority, but whatever He hears He will speak; and He will tell you things to come. **-John 16:13 (NKJV)**

I was reminded this week of how the Holy Spirit will let you know about 'things to come' in daily life. I was driving to work, and the Spirit was showing me about an issue at work. Sure enough, I ran into this situation and had to remind myself that the Lord already knows and has it under control. Stay open to hearing and receiving from Holy Spirit!

Please note: Holy Spirit is not an "IT" but rather "He."

Personal Reflection and Application:

_____

_____

_____

_____

_____

_____

_____

_____

_____

_____

REST

Saturday

Date: _____

Six days you shall do your work, and on the seventh day you shall rest, that your ox and your donkey may rest, and the son of your female servant and the stranger may be refreshed. **-Exodus 23:12 (NKJV)**

I'm simply encouraging you to have BALANCE in your life. When it's time for work, be diligent and efficient, but take time away from work to REST and truly be refreshed. Spend time in the presence of the CREATOR and enjoy His creation and blessings.

Personal Reflection and Application:

_____
_____
_____
_____
_____
_____
_____
_____
_____
_____
_____

LIFE

Sunday

Date: _____

These things I have spoken to you, that in Me you may have peace. In the world you will have tribulation; but be of good cheer, I have overcome the world. **-John 16:33 (NKJV)**

Life does not have to be perfect for you to enjoy it! As a matter of fact, life will not always go as planned. Make a decision to have peace and stay cheerful!

Personal Reflection and Application:

_____

_____

_____

_____

_____

_____

_____

_____

_____

_____

Weekend 6

"And they overcame him by the blood of the Lamb and by the word of their testimony, and they loved not their lives unto the death." -**Revelation 12:11 (NKJV)**

When seeking to draw closer to God, we defeat and overcome the enemy first through the blood of the Lamb Jesus Christ who grants us salvation, liberty, strength and power in abundance. Many believers may not realize that we also overcome the enemy through the sharing of our testimony. When we break free of strongholds in our lives, we release the power that they once had over us and we grant freedom to others. Through our confession, others can overcome by realizing that they are not alone in this walk of faith and that they too can overcome with the help of the Lord.

Contributor- Portavia Chandler, Epidemiologist

DIVINE PROTECTION

Friday

Date: _____

Psalm 91

Today, take a few moments and read Psalm 91. The Lord has given us divine protection. Almost nightly, just before I close my eyes, I say, "Thank you, Lord, for giving your angels charge over me that no evil shall befall me nor come near my dwelling." I have lived in several different states alone. While I do use wisdom and take the appropriate security precautions, I have peace of mind trusting that God will protect me. Stand on God's Word and pray for divine protection for yourself and others.

Personal Reflection and Application:

_____

_____

_____

_____

_____

_____

_____

_____

_____

_____

A NEW THING

Saturday

Date: _____

Behold, I will do a new thing; not it shall spring forth; shall ye not know it? I will even make a way in the wilderness and rivers in the desert. - **Isaiah 43:19 (KJV)**

I'm writing this devotional while I'm out of town this weekend. It occurred to me that sometimes you can't see the new thing that God is doing because of your everyday routine. Stepping away from your normal everyday life can give you a new perspective. The normal everyday tasks and 'to do list' aren't nagging at me, so I can focus more on the Lord. Focusing on Him allows me to download His wisdom and perspective on a situation. I can truly see that He is doing an awesome and new thing in my life! Focus on God and see the new thing that He is doing in your life!

Personal Reflection and Application:

_____

_____

_____

_____

_____

_____

_____

_____

_____

_____

VICTORY

Sunday

Date: _____

Oh, clap your hands, all you peoples! Shout to God with the voice of triumph! -**Psalm 47:1 (NKJV)**

As an act of faith, lift your hands and your voice unto the Lord. Praise Him for your VICTORY!

Personal Reflection and Application:

_____

_____

_____

_____

_____

_____

_____

_____

_____

_____

Weekend 7

Things are going to happen so fast your head will swim, one thing fast on the heels of the other. You won't be able to keep up. Everything will be happening at once—and everywhere you look, blessings! Blessings like wine pouring off the mountains and hills. **-Amos 9:13 (MSG)**

God's plan has been in existence since the foundation of the world. He knew where we would be at this very moment and He has just been waiting for us to get in position for His plan to fully manifest in our lives. So ready, set, go! Things are going to happen so fast. Keep up! God is up to something BIG in your life.

Contributor- Dr. Cecelia Jeffries "Dr. J", Speech Pathologist & Communication Coach, Owner of Concepts In Communication, LLC

WRITE THE VISION

Friday

Date: _____

Then the Lord answered me and said, "Write the vision and engrave it plainly on [clay] tablets so that the one who reads it will run. **Habakkuk 2:2 (Amp)**

The Word says to Write the Vision. Honestly, sometimes I have had to RE-WRITE the vision. As I pray and mediate on my petitions and the Word, I receive greater clarity and insight so that my vision becomes even more specific. If you don't have some sort of vision board, then start one. If you already have one, then revisit it and see if you need to add any details or make any changes. The vision provides you with a focal point. With a clear vision and focus, you are positioning yourself to receive instructions and direction.

Personal Reflection and Application:

_____

_____

_____

_____

_____

_____

_____

_____

_____

_____

LIVE ABUNDANTLY

Saturday

Date: _____

The thief does not come expect to steal, and to kill, and to destroy. I have come that they may have life, and that they may have it more abundantly. **-John 10:10 (NKJV)**

What will make your life more fulfilling? Do you want to volunteer, exercise, start a new hobby, spend more time with family/friends, launch a new business? Make a commitment today to have a more fulfilling life. Step out of your comfort zone and S-T-R-E-T-C-H! **Get a Life!**

Personal Reflection and Application:

_____

_____

_____

_____

_____

_____

_____

_____

_____

_____

_____

FRUITFUL

Sunday

Date: _____

Then it shall come to pass, because you listen to these judgments, and keep and do them, that the Lord your God will keep with you the covenant and the mercy which He swore to your fathers. And He will love you and bless you and multiply you; He will also bless the fruit of your womb and the fruit of your land, your grain and your new wine and your oil, the increase of your cattle and the offspring of your flock, in the land of which He swore to your fathers to give you. **-Deuteronomy 7:12-13 (NKJV)**

How do you have a fruitful and blessed life? Obedience! We have a covenant (an agreement) with God. Comply with the terms (obey) and receive the benefits!

Personal Reflection and Application:

_____
_____
_____
_____
_____
_____
_____
_____
_____
_____

Weekend 8

The blessing of the Lord, it maketh rich, and he add no sorrow with it. - **Proverbs 10:22 (KJV)**

This was a scripture given to me in 2014 by an anointed Man of God. Every time I read this scripture it provides strength and clarity in my daily walk on this righteous journey. At different times in my reflection on this scripture, it reveals different things. Today's nuggets: "It is He! I am the giver of all great things! It is only the blessing of God that gives joy, peace, and wealth. I repeat, there is no toil in the word of God." It reminds me of when I was younger, and my mother frequently reminded me to not bring home things that didn't belong to me. If it did not come from my mother, I could not accept it. Equally so, if it does not come from our Heavenly Father, we cannot accept it, we cannot bring it home with us. His blessing is everlasting and more than enough!

Contributor- Shameika L. Stokes, DSW. LCSW
Professor / Therapist /Advocate

CAST YOUR CARES

Friday

Date: _____

Therefore, the sisters sent to Him, saying, "Lord, behold, he whom You love is sick. **- John 11:3 (NKJV)**

Take the pressure off of yourself and remind God of His Word. Yes, Mary and Martha both loved their brother Lazarus but were limited in their abilities to directly help him. Instead, they reminded Jesus about His love for Lazarus. You shouldn't carry the burden of a situation or a person, even if it's a family member. When I pray for family members, I remind God that this person is His son or daughter, and therefore, HE is ultimately responsible for them – not me. Cast your cares upon the Lord and put Him in remembrance of His Word.

Personal Reflection and Application:

_____
_____
_____
_____
_____
_____
_____
_____
_____
_____

FAITH

Saturday

Date: _____

For in Christ Jesus neither circumcision nor uncircumcision avails anything, but faith working through love. **– Galatians 5:6 (NKJV)**

Fear and worry will cause you to doubt God. When you realize how much God loves you, then you can have faith that He will do everything that He promised.

God loves you, so have faith in Him!

Personal Reflection and Application:

_____

_____

_____

_____

_____

_____

_____

_____

_____

_____

_____

REST

Sunday

Date: _____

I will both lie down in peace, and sleep; For You alone, O Lord, make me dwell in safety. **-Psalm 4:8 (NKJV)**

It is vain for you to rise up early, to sit up late, to eat the bread of sorrows; *For* so He gives His beloved sleep. **-Psalm 127:2 (NKJV)**

I know - I know you have a long to do list and you are very busy BUT your physical body needs REST. How does this all connect? Worry and heavy emotions about life can rob you of your sleep and ability to relax. Trying to do everything is too taxing. What has God called you to do in this season? How efficient are you handling these tasks? It's so important to trust God and seek His wisdom because you need **REST**.

Personal Reflection and Application:

_____

_____

_____

_____

_____

_____

_____

_____

_____

_____

Weekend 9

I can do all things through Christ who strengthens me. Nevertheless, you have done well that you shared in my distress. **-Philippians 4:13-14 (NKJV)**

Too many times we experience great victories in Christ and become stagnant. This scripture does not say forget the bad things but forget all things and move forward. Walking with Him requires a constant forward progress until we hear well done thy good and faithful servant.

Contributor- Mrs. Rone Gold Washington, Teacher

VICTORY

Friday

Date: _____

For whatever is born of God overcomes the world. And this is the victory that has overcome the world- our faith. Who is he who overcomes the world, but he who believes that Jesus is the Son of God? **-I John 5:4-5 (NKJV)**

While we may look forward to the 'sweet by and by,' God wants us to have victory here in the earthly realm. Continue developing your faith through reading the Word and spending time with the Lord in prayer.

Faith = Victory!

Personal Reflection and Application:

_____

_____

_____

_____

_____

_____

_____

_____

_____

_____

_____

FRUITFUL

Saturday

Date: _____

I am the vine, you are the branches. He who abides in Me, and I in him, bears much fruit; for without Me you can do nothing. If anyone does not abide in Me, he is cast out as a branch and is withered; and they gather them and throw them into the fire, and they are burned. If you abide in Me, and My words abide in you, you will ask what you desire and it shall be done for you. By this My Father is glorified, that you bear much fruit; so you will be My disciples. **- John 15:5-8 (NKJV)**

To bear fruit or not to bear fruit? That is the question. Jesus gives us instructions on how to bear 'much fruit'. Abide means to stay or reside. It's important to stay in relationship with the Lord to have the blessed and productive life that God has for you.

Personal Reflection and Application:

_____
_____
_____
_____
_____
_____
_____
_____
_____
_____
_____

GRACE

Sunday

Date: _____

And lest I should be exalted above measure by the abundance of the revelations, a thorn in the flesh was given to me, a messenger of Satan to buffet me, lest I be exalted above measure. Concerning this thing I pleaded with the Lord three times that it might depart from me. And He said to me, "My grace is sufficient for you, for My strength is made perfect in weakness." Therefore most gladly I will rather boast in my infirmities, that the power of Christ may rest upon me. Therefore I take pleasure in infirmities, in reproaches, in needs, in persecutions, in distresses, for Christ's sake. For when I am weak, then I am strong. **– 2 Corinthians 12:7-10 (NKJV)**

Have you ever found yourself in a situation that wasn't 'ideal'? You may have prayed and asked God to change the situation but to no avail. Even if God doesn't change the situation, rest assured that He is with you. His grace covers and strengthens you.

Personal Reflection and Application:

_____

_____

_____

_____

_____

_____

_____

_____

_____

_____

Weekend 10

Being confident of this, that he who began a good work in you will carry it on to the completion until the day of Christ Jesus. - **Philippians 1:6 (NIV)**

How encouraging and uplifting it is to know that God is perfecting us for His call and service. He knows the plans that He has for us and if we cooperate with Him, He will reveal His plan to us and we will go from glory to glory in Him. We are His workmanship created in Christ Jesus for good works. It is His good pleasure to continue to perform His good work in us. Jesus said that these signs would follow the believer: In His name, we should cast out devils; speak with new tongues; and lay hands on the sick and see them recover. Expect God to do it and praise Him for it.

Contributor- Gloria G. Garvin, Educator

HEART

Friday

Date: _____

But others fell on good ground and yielded a crop: some a hundredfold, some sixty, some thirty. **-Matthew 13:8 (NKJV)**

I love this parable and how the Lord puts things into a context that we can comprehend. A farmer must put the good seed into fertile ground to get a harvest. God's Word is good seed and will produce. Now, the question is whether your heart is a good ground? Don't allow disappointment, delay, unforgiveness, or bitterness deplete your soil. Instead, prepare the soil of your heart with prayer, praise, hope, love and faith. A dear brother said, "Preparation is an indication of faith." When you can move pass a situation and expect God's blessing—the Word will produce victory in your life!

Personal Reflection and Application:

_____

_____

_____

_____

_____

_____

_____

_____

_____

_____

DELIVERED

Saturday

Date: _____

For if you remain completely silent at this time, relief and deliverance will arise for the Jews from another place, but you and your father's house will perish. Yet who knows whether you have come to the kingdom for *such* a time as this? **-Esther 4:14 (NKJV)**

God ensures that His people shall be delivered. The question is whether we will do our part and stay in a place of safety (obedience). Esther, an average everyday woman, was ordained by God to help save His people. When you are praying and seeking the Lord for His will, you have to recognize that your life is not an accident. You are at that job, attending that church, married to that man and mothering that child on purpose.

Personal Reflection and Application:

_____
_____
_____
_____
_____
_____
_____
_____
_____
_____
_____

PURPOSE

Sunday

Date: _____

For if you remain completely silent at this time, relief and deliverance will arise for the Jews from another place, but you and your father's house will perish. Yet who knows whether you have come to the kingdom for *such* a time as this? **-Esther 4:14 (NKJV)**

God ensures that His people shall be delivered. The question is whether we will do our part and stay in a place of safety (obedience). Esther, an average everyday woman, was ordained by God to help save His people. When you are praying and seeking the Lord for His will, you have to recognize that your life is not an accident.

For instance, my natural jobs include a spiritual assignment. I've had countless jobs where there is some female to whom I am supposed to minister. I remember my first job out of college. I was working as a receptionist. I had a degree and didn't want to work as receptionist but there was another administrative person across the hall. I was able to befriend her and help her get out of an abusive relationship and return to the things of God with her little girl. Your current positions and assignments are not an accident – God has a purpose!

Personal Reflection and Application:

_____

_____

_____

_____

_____

_____

_____

_____

Weekend 11

But I keep under my body, and bring it into subjection: lest that by any means, when I have preached to others, I myself should be a castaway. **-1 Corinthians 9:27 (KJV)**

This scripture keeps me grounded and sober in my day-to-day activities. It reminds me that as I minister, encourage, and pray for others that I must also spend time with God and study his word. This enables me to stay sensitive to His leading and always obey Him. If we don't the very things that we encourage others in, we can fall prey to.

Contributor- Dr. Crystal Gantt, Curriculum Coordinator

CORRECTION

Friday

Date: _____

For whom the LORD loves HE chastens, and scourges every son whom He receives **-Hebrews 12:6 (NKJV)**

Yes, even the Lord's correction is an expression of His love for you. Remember that He corrects you because He cares. It may not feel good, but it is beneficial because it keeps you on the path to a victorious life and righteousness. Receive God's loving correction.

Personal Reflection and Application:

_____
_____
_____
_____
_____
_____
_____
_____
_____
_____

LOVE

Saturday

Date: _____

By this all will know that you are My disciples, if you have love for one another. **-John 13:35 (NKJV)**

To advance the establishment of the Kingdom of God, you must receive His love and share it with others. In this way, others will see that you are a disciple of Christ.

Personal Reflection and Application:

_____

_____

_____

_____

_____

_____

_____

_____

_____

_____

HEART

Sunday

Date: _____

And when He had removed him, He raised up for them David as king, to whom also He gave testimony and said, 'I have found David the *son* of Jesse, a man after My *own* heart, who will do all My will.' **-Acts 13:22 (NKJV)**

If you know the story of David, you know that he was not perfect. Whenever he sinned against God, he confessed and repented. He had a heart to serve and please God. In turn, he was a man after God's own heart because he was committed to doing the will of God. You may not be perfect but strive to do God's will so you can be a woman after God's heart. Our aim should be to please God over everyone else!

Personal Reflection and Application:

_____

_____

_____

_____

_____

_____

_____

_____

_____

_____

Weekend 12

She gets up before dawn to prepare breakfast for her household and plan the day's work for her servant girls. (NLT)
She gets up while it is still night; she provides food for her family and portions for her female servants. (NIV) **-Proverbs 31:15**

We all as women desire and strive to be the Proverbs 31 Woman. Over the years, the Lord has used this scripture to minister to me. Yes, she was a diligent hard-working woman, BUT because she had help, she knew how to delegate responsibilities. She was not trying to do it ALL herself. Allow others to help you become God's Virtuous Woman.

Contributor- Yolonda C. Mason, Wife and Mom

SELF-WORTH

Friday

Date: _____

Who can find a virtuous wife? For her worth *is* far above rubies. - **Proverbs 31:10 (NKJV)**

I was talking to a friend this week about some recent challenges and disappoints that I faced. She reminded me of how valuable that I am as person. I found our conversation to be very encouraging. Remembering our self-worth helps us to keep our heads up despite our challenges and gives us the courage not to settle for less in our lives. In my career, I am grateful for my job, but I know I have more to offer, so I'm expecting new opportunities for promotion. Even when it comes to a mate, I don't expect him to be perfect, but I won't accept just anything either. One last note ... mistakes don't change your value or worth. When you are in Christ, He forgives and cleanses you. Your value is still far above rubies or any other precious gem.

Personal Reflection and Application:

_____

_____

_____

_____

_____

_____

_____

_____

_____

_____

CHARACTER

Saturday

Date: _____

The heart of her husband safely trusts her; so he will have no lack of gain. She does him good and not evil all the days of her life. **-Proverbs 31:11-12 (NKJV)**

Both married and single women, can learn from this wise woman. Whether it's a marriage, family relationship or a friendship, we have to be women of character and integrity. As Christian women, we should be the type of friend/family member/spouse that people's heart can trust. We need to show God's love through patience, support and prayer. The people in our lives should never have to worry about us gossiping about them or in any other way betraying their trust. We need to be considerate both in our words and actions towards those in our life.

Personal Reflection and Application:

_____

_____

_____

_____

_____

_____

_____

_____

_____

_____

_____

POTENTIAL

Sunday

Date: _____

Proverbs 31:10-31 (NKJV)

In Bible Study, we talked about the importance of tapping into your potential. The Proverbs 31 Woman truly tapped into her potential. She was business savvy (v.16), had a caring heart (v.20), creative (v.24), and organized (v.15) just to name a few of her qualities. She maximized her potential and created a blessed life for herself and for those around her — family and servants. Do you recognize your potential, qualities and gifts? Are you maximizing them? Keep Christ as your foundation and build with the tools that God has given you (v.30).

Personal Reflection and Application:

_____

_____

_____

_____

_____

_____

_____

_____

_____

_____

Weekend 13

"Stand fast therefore in the liberty by which Christ has made us free, and do not be entangled again with a yoke of bondage." - **Galatians 5:1 (NKJV)**

Recently, someone close to me accused me of lying. To make matters worse, instead of discussing the "lie" with me, the person told other people, including someone whose approval I was subconsciously seeking (The Holy Spirit showed me this later). I felt like my integrity and character were being attacked, however, they took a back seat to other people's perception of me. One of my first thoughts was "what would people think??" I wanted to defend myself but at that time, God said No. I got mad because I did not want people to think less of me, think that I actually lied, or that I could not be trusted. Using that situation God reminded me of two things. First, He knew the truth and His approval is all I need. Second, I will continue to be in bondage, a slave to people (allowing their approval to dictate my thoughts and behavior) if I choose to continue to seek their approval and always try to please them. Christ has already made me free; I no longer have to be bound by people. Being in bondage, a slave to the approval of others, is a choice. Today, I chose to be delivered from people. Today, I chose to "Stand fast therefore in the liberty by which Christ has made [me] free, and [to] not be entangled again with a yoke of bondage" (Galatians 5:1). I choose to walk as a free woman in Christ, knowing "therefore if the Son makes you free, you shall be free indeed" (John 8:36 NKJV); and if you are in any type of bondage, especially to people, I encourage you to do same.

Contributor- Bry-Anne E. Jones, MSW, LCSW

PERFECT LOVE

Friday

Date: _____

There is no fear in love; but perfect love casts out fear, because fear involves torment. But he who fears has not been made perfect in love. **-1 John 4:18 (NKJV)**

There is no need to walk in fear—the Lord's love for you is perfect and complete. To overcome fear, focus on and receive God's love for you. Fear paralyzes, but God's love will energize and enable you to have a joyful and peaceful life.

Personal Reflection and Application:

_____

_____

_____

_____

_____

_____

_____

_____

_____

SPIRIT

Saturday
Date: _____

If you love Me, keep My commandments. And I will pray the Father, and He will give you another Helper, that He may abide with you forever—the Spirit of truth, whom the world cannot receive, because it neither sees Him nor knows Him; but you know Him, for He dwells with you and will be in you. **-John 14:15-17 (NKJV)**

These are the words of Jesus! He is speaking about the Holy Spirit. Notice Jesus does not refer to the Holy Spirit as an 'it' but rather 'He'—the Third Person of the Godhead. He is our Helper, dwells with us and leads us into all truth so that we fulfill God's purpose! You don't have to journey alone, let the Spirit of God help you!

Personal Reflection and Application:

_____

PEACE

Sunday

Date: _____

You will keep *him* in perfect peace, *Whose* mind *is* stayed *on You,* Because he trusts in You. **-Isaiah 26:3 (NKJV)**

Make a decision to stay focused on and trust in God. In the midst of any situation, you can have peace. Your peace does not depend on circumstances. Life will change but God is consistent and can always keep you in peace.

Personal Reflection and Application:

_____

_____

_____

_____

_____

_____

_____

_____

_____

_____

Weekend 14

It shall come to pass

That before they call,

I will answer;

And while they are still speaking, I will hear.

Isaiah 65:24 (NKJV)

I thank God that He always hears my prayers. He changes my desires to His desires. He answers my prayers. **-Barbara Wilson, Mother of Capresha Caldwell**

PEACE

Friday

Date: _____

God is our refuge and strength, an ever-present help in trouble. **-Psalm 46:1 (NIV)**

Don't worry or fear! Keep your peace! Even in troubling situations, God will help you. He will protect you and give you the strength you need to overcome.

Personal Reflection and Application:

_____
_____
_____
_____
_____
_____
_____
_____
_____
_____
_____

MIND

Saturday

Date: _____

And do not be conformed to this world, but be transformed by the renewing of your mind, that you may prove what is that good and acceptable and perfect will of God. **-Romans 12:2 (NIV)**

Do you want to see a change in your life? Examine your mindset. Are your thoughts in alignment with the Word of God? Change your mind and change your life!

Personal Reflection and Application:

_____
_____
_____
_____
_____
_____
_____
_____
_____
_____
_____

DIVINE PROTECTION

Sunday

Date: _____

The fruit of the righteous *is a* tree of life, and he who wins souls *is* wise.
Proverbs 11:30 (NKJV)

We should tell others about how awesome Jesus is in our lives! People that you encounter come from different backgrounds with various experiences. You need God's wisdom to approach that person properly! I remember a lady that shared this story about how she led a person to Christ who was working in the drive through. In that situation, you don't have a lot of time to figure out the person! She received the wisdom of God and it happened in just a few short minutes—Wow! Ask God to give you the wisdom to win your loved ones, friends, and even strangers to Christ.

Personal Reflection and Application:

_____
_____
_____
_____
_____
_____
_____
_____
_____
_____

Weekend 15

Purpose Blockers

So too, faith, if it does not have works [to back it up], is by itself dead [inoperative and ineffective]. **-James 2:17 (AMP)**

If you find yourself walking in circles you probably have an issue with being easily distracted or procrastination. Some of the same habits demonstrated when it comes to completing personal goals are typically the same habits keeping you from your purpose. Examine your heart and ask God to reveal the root cause of your purpose blockers. God will give you the desires of your heart (Psalm 37:4). However, you must work for it.

Contributor- Shanita L. Rogers, Author, Public Speaker & Moderator

ENCOURAGEMENT

Friday

Date: _____

May our Lord Jesus Christ himself and God our Father, who loved us and by his grace gave us eternal encouragement and good hope, encourage your hearts and strengthen you in every good deed and word. -2 **Thessalonians 2:16–17 (NIV)**

Be encouraged, and let your hearts be strengthened in every situation. He loves you. God loves you, and He has a good plan for your life. Listen and be open to the Holy Spirit's guidance. (Jeremiah 29:11)

Personal Reflection and Application:

_____

_____

_____

_____

_____

_____

_____

_____

_____

_____

Capresha Caldwell

PATIENCE

Saturday

Date: _____

For the vision is yet for an appointed time; But at the end it will speak, and it will not lie. **Though it tarries**, wait for it; Because it will surely comely. It will not tarry. - **Habakkuk 2:3 (NKJV) (emphasize added)**

Sister – waiting is a part of the journey! It takes time to accomplish your goals and receive the full manifestation of your prayers. The wait doesn't take God by surprise. He has already informed us about the wait (tarry) and encouraged us that *it will* come to pass. Take time to refocus, regroup and refresh then continue Moving Forward in Jesus name!

Personal Reflection and Application:

_____
_____
_____
_____
_____
_____
_____
_____
_____
_____

ALL IS WELL

Sunday

Date: _____

Please run now to meet her, and say to her, 'Is it well with you? It is well with your husband? Is it well with the child?' And she answered, "It is well." **-2 Kings 4:26 (NKJV)**

IT IS WELL and some translations say ALL IS WELL. This is one of my favorite stories in the Bible. The Shunammite just experienced the promise of God – her son – die in her arms. But she refused to accept the death of God's promise and her heart's desire. In the midst of the situation, she released her faith by her Words and Actions. She said It is Well and she went to get the Prophet to pray over her son. Don't let the promises of God die in your life! Because of her faith and corresponding action, her son was resurrected. The promise of God was alive and well in her life!

Personal Reflection and Application:

_____

_____

_____

_____

_____

_____

_____

_____

_____

_____

_____

Weekend 16

Psalm 23 (NKJV)

The LORD *is* my shepherd; I shall not want. He makes me to lie down in green pastures; He leads me beside the still waters. He restores my soul; He leads me in the paths of righteousness for His name's sake. Yea, though I walk through the valley of the shadow of death, I will fear no evil; for You *are* with me; Your rod and Your staff, they comfort me. You prepare a table before me in the presence of my enemies; You anoint my head with oil; my cup runs over. Surely goodness and mercy shall follow me all the days of my life; and I will dwell in the house of the LORD forever.

The Lord has been with me through the ups and downs, happy and sad times. I have seen a lot in my life. I am strong in God. I have lived a good life and I thank Him. **-Molly Ward, Grandmother of Capresha Caldwell**

LOVE

Friday

Date: _____

For I am persuaded that neither death nor life, nor angels nor principalities nor powers, nor things present nor things to come, nor height nor depth, nor any other created thing, shall be able to separate us from the **love of God which is in Christ Jesus our Lord**. - **Romans 8:38–39 (NKJV)(emphasize added)**

God's love is greater than any challenge that you will face. In whatever circumstance or situation that you may encounter, continue to cling to and rely on God's love for you! Daily reminding yourself about God's love will encourage your heart and give you the strength to move forward.

Personal Reflection and Application:

_____
_____
_____
_____
_____
_____
_____
_____
_____
_____
_____

ABIDE

Saturday

Date: _____

And we have known and believed the love that God has for us. God is love, and he who abides in love abides in God, and God in him. - **1 John 4:16 (NKJV)**

GOD IS LOVE (1 John 4:8). Based on the word of God, you can know and can wholeheartedly say that God loves you. As you continue through this year, continue to rest and dwell in God's love, confident that He who is love is abiding in you. If anything tries to pull you from the love of God or convince you otherwise, be diligent to stay focused on God's love.

Personal Reflection and Application:

_____
_____
_____
_____
_____
_____
_____
_____
_____
_____
_____
_____

SPIRIT

Sunday

Date: _____

Do not cast me from your presence or take your Holy Spirit from me. - **Psalm 51:11 (NIV)**

We have to have a heart for the Lord. It's great to have blessings but our focus must stay on God and His faithfulness. Our heart's cry should be for the presence of the Lord!

Personal Reflection and Application:

_____
_____
_____
_____
_____
_____
_____
_____
_____
_____

Weekend 17

"let us lay aside every weight, and the sin which so easily ensnares *us,...*" - **Hebrews 12:1-2 (NKJV)**

Naturally speaking, I have overpacked. Too many shoes, too many clothes... just too much. There have been too many times I had to take things out of my luggage and put in my husband's. Too many things. I am telling you today where you are going... you can't take everything and everyone with you. Even on a plane when your luggage is too heavy you either pay extra or must leave it behind. Friends, your next move is going to require some lighter weight.

If not, the cost may be too much to carry those extra things like unforgiveness, offense or lying with you. Commit today to unpack your bags.

Contributor- Roshanda "The Rosho" Pratt, First Lady of Visibility

SPIRIT

Friday

Date: _____

But the Helper, the Holy Spirit, whom the Father will send in My name, He will teach you all things, and bring to your remembrance all things that I said to you – **John 14:26 (NKJV)**

The Holy Spirit is a person and He is our helper. You are not alone on this Christian Journey. I remember studying for the bar exam. Previously, I had failed the test and it was an enormous amount of material to cover. Since I had studied the different topics, I began to pray and confess that the Holy Spirit would bring everything to my remembrance. I passed— Glory to God! On numerous occasions, the Holy Spirit brought to my remembrance the faithfulness of God in my life.

Personal Reflection and Application:

_____
_____
_____
_____
_____
_____
_____
_____
_____
_____

TRUTH

Saturday

Date: _____

However, when He, the Spirit of truth, has come, He will guide you into all truth; for He will not speak on His own *authority,* but whatever He hears He will speak; and He will tell you things to come. He will glorify Me, for He will take of what is Mine and declare *it* to you. – **John 16:13-14 (NKJV)**

In these scriptures, Jesus is speaking to His disciples and preparing them for his departure. He gives us greater insight about the Holy Spirit. He, the Holy Spirit, guides us into all truth and tells us things to come. Prayer and confessions are both important. In prayer, ask God to guide you into the truth of any situation by His Holy Spirit. Confessions are more than about just speaking positive words, but it's important that we speak God's Word. This scripture is the basis of one of my confessions of faith, "The Holy Spirit will lead me and guide me into all truth and show me things to come."

Personal Reflection and Application:

_____
_____
_____
_____
_____
_____
_____
_____
_____
_____
_____

WISDOM

Sunday

Date: _____

For the Lord gives wisdom; From His mouth *come* knowledge and understanding; – **Proverbs 2:6 (NKJV)**

It's valuable to have mentors and other experienced and knowledgeable people around to consult. But the ultimate 'mentor' and guide is the Lord. His wisdom is perfect and available to you! Ask in faith and you will receive! I can think of times when I just didn't know what to do and asked God for wisdom. I was moving from South Carolina to Tennessee and needed to get rid of my furniture but couldn't afford to just give it away. God gave me the right person and some insight on the best deal to make. It was close to my move time, and I was thankful that it all worked out!

Personal Reflection and Application:

_____
_____
_____
_____
_____
_____
_____
_____
_____
_____

Weekend 18

Predestinated: To appoint, decree, ordain, declare, determine, or specify.

For whom he did foreknow, he also did predestinate to be conformed to the image of his Son, that he might be the firstborn among many brethren. Moreover, whom he did predestinate, them he also called: and whom he called, them he also justified: and whom he justified, them he also glorified. - **Romans 8:29-30 (KJV)**

There have been several times in my life when I have faced adversity, bad circumstances, disappointments, and heartache. There have been times I felt like I had no control of my own destiny or control of the outcome of events. I asked God why and wondered if I caused the turmoil myself based on bad decisions. I have spent countless hours thinking to myself "what if" and then one day I heard a message preached on the topic "Predestinated," which ultimately changed my perspective on life. The revelation came to me that my life has been predestinated by God; and He knew me before the foundations of the earth. Therefore, despite the situations or circumstances I might face I know my life has been predestinated by God, who has appointed, decreed, ordained, specified, declared, and determined the final outcome of my life.

Contributor- Darice Stephenson, Certified Holistic Health Coach

LIFE

Friday

Date: _____

I shall not die, but live, and declare the works of the LORD. – **Psalm 118:17 (NKJV)**

Don't allow anything to hinder your progress, discourage you or bring you down. You have encountered previous disappointments, frustrations and maybe any failures but you still have opportunities and hope. Make a decision to live out loud and go forth boldly in what God has called you to do. Your courageous actions of fulfilling God's purpose for your life speaks volumes of His goodness. You are alive, so live!

Personal Reflection and Application:

_____
_____
_____
_____
_____
_____
_____
_____
_____

MIND

Saturday

Date: _____

Casting down arguments and every high thing that exalts itself against the knowledge of God, bringing every thought into captivity to the obedience of Christ. **-2 Corinthians 10:5 (NKJV)**

God has given you control of your thought life! You do not have to entertain negative, self-defeating thoughts. Reject those thoughts and replace them with what the Word of God says about you!

Personal Reflection and Application:

_____
_____
_____
_____
_____
_____
_____
_____
_____
_____
_____

REST

Sunday

Date: _____

And He said, "My Presence will go with you, and I will give you rest." - **Exodus 33:14 (NKJV)**

You may be starting a new and exciting journey or facing a challenging path. You may even be somewhere in between. Do not allow your emotions or mind to be overwhelmed. Just remember the Lord is with you, so REST in HIM as you continue moving forward!

Personal Reflection and Application:

_____

_____

_____

_____

_____

_____

_____

_____

_____

_____

_____

Weekend 19

Now may He who supplies seed to the sower, and bread for food, supply and multiply the seed you have sown and increase the fruits of your righteousness. **2 Corinthians 9:10**

Giving provides seed for the Kingdom and it compels God to multiply your seed back to you to meet your needs. When circumstances get tough you should not stop giving. When you stop giving you stop the flow of God's blessings in your life.

Contributor- Anselita D. Newkirk, First Lady, Centrifuge Church

ROLE MODEL

Friday

Date: _____

Therefore be imitators of God as dear children. And walk in love, as Christ also has loved us and given Himself for us, an offering and a sacrifice to God for a sweet-smelling aroma. **-Ephesians 5:1-2 (NKJV)**

In today's society, many people want to imitate entertainers and athletes. As a Christian, you should imitate God and walk in love.

Personal Reflection and Application:

_____
_____
_____
_____
_____
_____
_____
_____
_____
_____

ETERNAL LIFE

Saturday

Date: _____

By this we know love, because He laid down His life for us. And we also ought to lay down our lives for the brethren. **-1 John 3:16 (NKJV)**

To lay down our lives for the brethren, we must abandon what we want in our lives and live life as Christ modeled it for us. There is no need to wonder, worry, or fret—Jesus loves us!

Personal Reflection and Application:

_____
_____
_____
_____
_____
_____
_____
_____
_____
_____

REST

Sunday

Date: _____

Come to Me, all you who labor and are heavy laden, and I will give you rest. Take My yoke upon you and learn from Me, for I am gentle and lowly in heart, and you will find rest for your souls. For My yoke is easy and My burden is light. **-Matthew 11:28-30 (NKJV)**

You don't have to wait to exhale. Jesus is giving you an invitation to bring all the cares of life to Him. Salvation is not just about your spirit but it's also about your soul (mind, will and emotions). The Lord has a better way that is both easy and light. Go to Him in prayer about all of your concerns and submit to His way.

Personal Reflection and Application:

_____
_____
_____
_____
_____
_____
_____
_____
_____
_____
_____

Weekend 20

If I were in your shoes, I'd go straight to God, I'd throw myself on the mercy of God. After all, he's famous for great and unexpected acts; there's no end to his surprises. **-Job 5:8-9 (MSG)**

This is a scripture that I use often when I'm praying for others to encourage them not to go anywhere, to anybody, but to go to God. He knows exactly what we need, when we need it, how it needs to be done. He is always right there, and he is full of surprises. We will be simply amazed at how he handles the situation. Go straight to God!

Contributor- Dr. Cecelia Jeffries "Dr. J", Speech Pathologist & Communication Coach, Owner of Concepts In Communication, LLC

FAITH

Friday

Date: _____

So, when Jesus came, He found that he had already been in the tomb four days. Now Bethany was near Jerusalem, about two miles away. And many of the Jews had joined the women around Martha and Mary, to comfort them concerning their brother. Now Martha, as soon as she heard that Jesus was coming, went and met Him, but Mary was sitting in the house. Now Martha said to Jesus, "Lord, if You had been here, my brother would not have died. But even now I know that whatever You ask of God, God will give You." **-John 11:17-22**

Place close attention to verse 22. Through our words we release our faith. In the midst of a great lost, Martha had faith in God. Jesus performed a miracle and resurrected Lazarus! This year choose to have faith in God, speak faith over the situation and receive miracles!

Personal Reflection and Application:

_____

_____

_____

_____

_____

_____

_____

_____

_____

_____

_____

BLESSINGS

Saturday

Date: _____

v.8 - 10 Now it happened one day that Elisha went to Shunem, where there *was* a notable woman, and she persuaded him to eat some food. So it was, as often as he passed by, he would turn in there to eat some food. And she said to her husband, "Look now, I know this *is* a holy man of God, who passes by us regularly. Please, let us make a small upper room on the wall; and let us put a bed for him there, and a table and a chair and a lampstand; so it will be, whenever he comes to us, he can turn in there." v. 14 So he said, "What then *is* to be done for her?" And Gehazi answered, "Actually, she has no son, and her husband is old." v.17 But the woman conceived, and bore a son when the appointed time had come, of which Elisha had told her. **-2 Kings 4:8 – 37**

This is one of my favorite women! Please read entire passage. When I was in college, I had an opportunity to minister about the Shunammite Woman in the RRAW (Restored Resurrected Anointed Women of God) Bible Study. That was over 20 years ago but this story continues to inspire me! She was financially secure but there are some things money can't buy. You can't buy peace or a sound mind with money, but God has that available to you. She used her means to be a blessing and this act of being unselfish positioned her to receive the desire of her heart. You are blessed to be a blessing. When you open your hand and heart to help others, you are positioned to receive blessings. Her husband was older, and therefore, she was unable to have a child. However, she recognized that Elisha was a man God and honored him. In return, she received the desire of her heart.

Personal Reflection and Application:

_____
_____
_____
_____
_____
_____
_____
_____

OBEY

Sunday

Date: _____

But Samuel replied: "Does the LORD delight in burnt offerings and sacrifices as much as in obeying the LORD? To obey is better than sacrifice, and to heed is better than the fat of rams. **-1 Samuel 15:22 (NIV)**

If we want to please God, we must obey Him. We need to obey the written Word of God and the internal promptings of the Holy Spirit. It's not always 'convenient' and sometimes we would rather do the opposite. But our love for God and desire to please Him gives us the strength to be obedient. It's about developing our relationship with the Lord and showing Him that He can trust us, and He is our priority! Trust and obey God!

Personal Reflection and Application:

_____
_____
_____
_____
_____
_____
_____
_____
_____
_____

Weekend 21

As Jesus and his disciples were on their way, he came to a village where a woman named Martha opened her home to him. She had a sister called Mary, who sat at the Lord's feet listening to what he said. **-Luke 10:38 – 39 (NIV)**

What an honor and privilege to have direct access to Jesus – to have Him in your home. Mary recognized how precious this opportunity was and gave her attention to Him. You have direct access to the Lord through prayer and reading the Bible. Mary probably had a 'To-Do List,' but she pushed it aside to focus on Jesus. In the midst of all your errands and goals, choose to have quality time with the Lord – sit at His feet and listen to His Word!

REFUGE

Friday

Date: _____

God is our refuge and strength [mighty and impenetrable], a very present and well-proved help in trouble. **- Psalm 46:1 (AMP)**

What a week – God is so faithful! Have you ever had a situation when you needed God to move quickly?! Well, I had that type of experience this week. God met me at my point of need and the blessing manifested within 24 hours – thank you Lord! As the 'Old Folk' say – He will make a way out of no way. I could not see the solution, but God's provision was already in place. Trust God and continue moving forward!

Personal Reflection and Application:

_____
_____
_____
_____
_____
_____
_____
_____
_____
_____

LOVE

Saturday

Date: _____

We love Him because He first loved us. **- 1 John 4:19 (NKJV)**

God loved you FIRST! He initiated a love relationship with you. He knows everything about you, and He loves you despite your faults. Normally, in a relationship, you have to do something to "earn" love— but not with God. You didn't have to earn it, and you cannot stop it, even if you tried. His love is unconditional. By accepting Christ, you connect with God. Your most important relationship is with God through Christ. Accept His love and respond with love.

Personal Reflection and Application:

_____
_____
_____
_____
_____
_____
_____
_____
_____
_____
_____
_____

PEACE

Sunday

Date: _____

Then He said to the woman, "Your faith has saved you. Go in peace."
-Luke 7:50 (NKJV)

If you begin reading at Verse 36, you will see that this woman was considered a sinner. I know that's not a popular term in our society today but continue to read through verse 50. She recognized Jesus and worshiped Him and received both forgiveness and peace. Don't let any mistakes from your past haunt you and prevent you from receiving the Lord's forgiveness and peace!

Personal Reflection and Application:

_____
_____
_____
_____
_____
_____
_____
_____
_____
_____
_____

Weekend 22

The thief comes only in order to kill, steal, and destroy. I have come in order that you might have life - life in all of its fullness.
- John 10:10 (GNT)

What a familiar scripture; however, this scripture had become so familiar to me that I failed to realize and walk in all my benefits. God came to give us life in all of its fullness and everything concerning our lives. This includes fullness of health, finances, favor, peace, wisdom, discernment, and the list goes on and on. Daily we should be walking in the benefits God came to give us. Start walking in your fullness.

Contributor- Charmain Jones, Educator

VICTORY

Friday

Date: _____

But thanks be to God, who gives us the victory through our Lord Jesus Christ. **-1 Corinthians 15:57 (NKJV)**

Celebrate the VICTORIES in your life! God can give you victory in the face of all opposition and circumstances. Whatever you encounter, trust God for the victory!

Personal Reflection and Application:

_____

_____

_____

_____

_____

_____

_____

_____

_____

_____

Capresha Caldwell

FRUITFUL

Saturday

Date: _____

And God blessed them, saying, "Be fruitful and multiply, and fill the waters in the seas, and let birds multiply on the earth." **- Genesis 1:22 (NKJV)**

God has blessed us to be productive and experience good results. If you have areas in your life that seem barren, continue to stand in faith knowing that God has already blessed you. Rest assured that you will see the results...the fruits of your labor.

Personal Reflection and Application:

_____
_____
_____
_____
_____
_____
_____
_____
_____
_____
_____

TRUST

Sunday

Date: _____

(v.11-12) So I came to Jerusalem and was there three days. Then I arose in the night, I and a few men with me; I told no one what my God had put in my heart to do at Jerusalem; nor was there any animal with me, except the one on which I rode. (v.16) And the officials did not know where I had gone or what I had done; I had not yet told the Jews, the priests, the nobles, the officials, or the others who did the work.
- Nehemiah 2:11-12, 16 (NKJV)

When God places something in your heart, do not be too quick to tell others. Take the time to pray for clarity and position yourself to receive instructions from the Lord. Trust God to lead you to who and when to share His deposits in your heart.

Personal Reflection and Application:

_____
_____
_____
_____
_____
_____
_____
_____
_____
_____
_____

Weekend 23

Change

(v.12-14) On the day following, when they had come away from Bethany, He was hungry. And seeing in the distance a fig tree [covered] with leaves, He went to see if He could find any [fruit] on it [for in the fig tree the fruit appears at the same time as the leaves]. But when He came up to it, He found nothing but leaves, for the fig season had not yet come. And He said to it, No one ever again shall eat fruit from you. And His disciples were listening [to what He said]. (v.20-21) In the morning, when they were passing along, they noticed that the fig tree was withered [completely] away to its roots. And Peter remembered and said to Him, Master, look! The fig tree which You doomed has withered away! **- Mark 11:12-14, 20-21 - (AMPC)**

If you want to truly make a permanent change, deal with the root of the issue. Take time to prayerfully reflect and understand the true origin of an issue. Ask God to help you understand and identify the true cause. God reveals and heals!

MIND

Friday

Date: _____

You will keep *him* in perfect peace, Whose mind is stayed on *You*, Because he trusts in You. **-Isaiah 26:3(NKJV)**

The other day I encountered a stressful situation that I found to be overwhelming. Once I stepped away from the situation and refocused on the Lord, I was able to experience God's peace. Make sure you are focused on HIM!

Personal Reflection and Application:

_____
_____
_____
_____
_____
_____
_____
_____
_____
_____
_____
_____

LIFE

Saturday

Date: _____

The thief comes only in order to steal and kill and destroy. I came that they may have *and* enjoy life, and have it in abundance (to the full, till it overflows). **-Isaiah 26:3(NKJV)**

Jesus came that you can have a good earthly life and eternal life! Take advantage of the opportunities that you have to enjoy life. Even in the midst of an imperfect situation, find the bright spot! One week, I was in Philadelphia for a business trip. The hotel that I was staying in was clean but outdated. Normally, I would just endure for the week but not this time. I found a new hotel and rolled my luggage down the street. Why? Because I wanted to enjoy this business trip as much as possible and the new hotel made me happy!

Personal Reflection and Application:

_____
_____
_____
_____
_____
_____
_____
_____
_____
_____
_____

DIVINE PROTECTION

Sunday

Date: _____

He who dwells in the secret place of the Most High Shall abide under the shadow of the Almighty. I will say of the LORD, "He is my refuge and my fortress; My God, in Him I will trust." **- Psalm 91:1-2 (NKJV)**

I encourage you to read Psalm 91. Read about the divine protection of the Lord! God is your refuge and your fortress. Refuge is defined as shelter, protection, or safety. Fortress is defined as a place of exceptional security. Whether it's a physical, mental or emotional attack, the Lord is your refuge.

Personal Reflection and Application:

_____
_____
_____
_____
_____
_____
_____
_____
_____
_____
_____

Weekend 24

Not Guilty!

There is now no condemnation [no guilty verdict, no punishment] for those who are in Christ Jesus [who believe in Him as personal Lord and savior} -**Romans 8:1 (AMP)**

Some of the greatest burdens that people carry are the burdens of guilt. Once you repent you must forgive yourself. You are not the sin that you once committed. No longer do you have to carry the shame associated with your past. Christ came to redeem and set you free! You are not guilty!

Contributor- Shanita L. Rogers, Author, Public Speaker & Moderator

LOVE

Friday

Date: _____

Grace, mercy, and peace will be with you from God the Father and from the Lord Jesus Christ, the Son of the Father, in truth and love. **-2 John 1:3 (NKJV)**

We all need grace, mercy, and peace. Through God's love, you can receive everything that you need. Thank God for His love!

Personal Reflection and Application:

_____

_____

_____

_____

_____

_____

_____

_____

_____

_____

Capresha Caldwell

WISDOM

Saturday

Date: _____

If any of you lacks **wisdom**, let him ask of God, who gives to all liberally and without reproach, and it will be given to him. **-James 1:5 (NKJV)**

Wisdom is the principal thing; *Therefore* get wisdom. And in all your getting, get understanding. **-Proverbs 4:7 (NKJV)**

I was reading a commentary that stated wisdom was the whispered Word from God which directs us into the right path, and it must be our priority. We must seek God's wisdom in every area of our lives. I remember even in law school receiving the wisdom of God which enabled me to graduate. Is there a situation in which you need God's wisdom?

Personal Reflection and Application:

_____

_____

_____

_____

_____

_____

_____

_____

_____

_____

_____

HEART

Sunday

Date: _____

Keep your heart with all diligence,
For out it *spring* the issues of life.
-Proverbs 4:23 (NKJV)

Above all else, guard your affections.
For they influence everything else in your life.
-Proverbs 4:23 (TLB)

YOU have to be wise and diligent in guarding your heart. You must recognize how instrumental your heart is to your overall well-being. God is intentional—I am speaking to you from an emotional and spiritual perspective but look at this analogy—your physical body cannot function without a heart. You can survive without extremities (limb) or functions (sight/hearing) but you must have a heart to live! Keep your heart healthy so that you can enjoy life!

Personal Reflection and Application:

_____
_____
_____
_____
_____
_____
_____
_____
_____
_____

Weekend 25

This is GOD's Message, the God who made earth, made it livable and lasting, known everywhere as GOD: 'Call to me and I will answer you. I'll tell you marvelous and wondrous things that you could never figure out on your own.' -**Jeremiah 33: 2-3 (MSG)**

Seeking is one of the things that God encourages us to do as we make our way on this journey. But just seeking alone is not what He intends for us to do, so He says to call onto Him and then, lookout. He will show up and show out just for us, giving us information we could have never figured out on our own.

Contributor- Dr. Cecelia Jeffries "Dr. J", Speech Pathologist & Communication Coach, Owner of Concepts In Communication, LLC

FAITH

Friday

Date: _____

And she said, "Yes, Lord, yet even the little dogs eat the crumbs which fall from their masters' table." Then Jesus answered and said to her, 'O woman, great is your faith! Let it be to you as you desire." And her daughter was healed from that very hour. **-Matthew 15:27-28**

Whenever you read the entire passage referenced above (Matthew 15:21-28), you will see that she cried out to Jesus. Initially, He didn't respond to her (v.23). When He did respond, His focus wasn't on her. However, this woman was very witty and determined! She responded in Faith to Jesus. Her daughter was demon-possessed and needed deliverance (v.22)! She was willing to settle for crumbs, but Jesus gave her exactly what she asked for – deliverance for her daughter. You don't have to settle; He wants you to have the desires of your heart! Faith produces in your life and in the life of your loved ones!

Personal Reflection and Application:

_____
_____
_____
_____
_____
_____
_____
_____
_____
_____
_____

TEMPTATION

Saturday

Date: _____

And the lords of the Philistines came up to her and said to her, "Entice him, and find out where his great strength *lies*, and by what *means* we may overpower him, that we may bind him to afflict him; and every one of us will give you eleven hundred *pieces* of silver." So Delilah said to Samson, "Please tell me where your great strength *lies*, and with what you may be bound to afflict you." **- Judges 16:5-6 (NKJV)**

Men sought to destroy Samson and recognized that Delilah could help them. They offered her what I call a "dirty deal." She instantly accepted and started working her plan. The scriptures don't reflect Delilah having a moment of reflection or heavy conscious about undermining Samson. She gave her body to make money and this was simply another method to get money. What's on the inside of her that allowed her to agree to this deal without any trepidation? Money may be her area of temptation, but we will have to ensure that we don't have any areas of temptation. While we are striving to live for the Lord, it's important to stay on guard for areas of temptation. If we get into a place where we are willing to participate in questionable activity, then that's time for a self-check. What areas of temptation do you need to remain aware?

Personal Reflection and Application:

_____
_____
_____
_____
_____
_____
_____
_____
_____
_____

GRACE

Sunday

Date: _____

Let us therefore come boldly to the throne of grace, that we may obtain mercy and find grace to help in time of need. -**Hebrews 4:16 (NKJV)**

God's grace is always available to you. Yes, you can boldly go into the throne room in the name of Jesus! Do not allow anyone or any situation to tell you otherwise. He has given you an open invitation. Receive the mercy and grace that you need!

Personal Reflection and Application:

_____
_____
_____
_____
_____
_____
_____
_____
_____
_____

Weekend 26

Trust in the LORD with all your heart, and lean not on your own understanding; In all your ways acknowledge Him, And He shall direct your paths. **-Proverbs 3:5-6 (NKJV)**

Trust & Believe: Trusting God is something that happens when we develop a relationship with Him. Trust means to rely on the integrity, strength, ability, surety of a person or thing. Believing in God is having confidence in the truth of His word. Believing means to have confidence in the truth, the existence, or the reliability without proof. Trusting and Believing are both required in the Kingdom of God, the only difference is Trust in the natural can be broken. Believing in something or someone can be changed based on understanding. I have understood things differently and found that what I once believed had to change once I had a better understanding. We must first Trust and Believe, when we apply both Trust and Believing to our lives, the word tells us God will prove Himself faithful.

Contributor- Darice Stephenson, Certified Holistic Health Coach

LOVE

Friday

Date: _____

And now abide faith, hope, love, these three; but the greatest of these is love. **-1 Corinthians 13:13 (NKJV)**

To help us understand this scripture, let's do a comparison. In Hebrews 11:6, the Word says that without FAITH, it's IMPOSSIBLE to please God. In Hebrews 6:19, the Word states that HOPE is the ANCHOR of the soul. In today's scripture, we read that LOVE is the GREATEST of these three. God is serious about His love for you, your love for Him and your love for others.

Personal Reflection and Application:

_____
_____
_____
_____
_____
_____
_____
_____
_____
_____

MIND

Saturday

Date: _____

Finally, brethren, whatever things are true, whatever things *are* noble, whatever things *are* just, whatever things are pure, whatever things *are* lovely, whatever things *are* of good report, if *there is* any virtue and if *there is* anything praiseworthy—meditate on these things. - **Philippians 4:8 (NKJV)**

I like something that Joyce Meyers says (paraphrasing) - think about what you are thinking about. To me, that is such a profound statement. Your thought impacts your actions, words, emotions and ultimately your life. You need to be aware of your thoughts and how they influence your life!

Personal Reflection and Application:

_____
_____
_____
_____
_____
_____
_____
_____
_____
_____
_____
_____

WISDOM

Sunday

Date: _____

If any of you lacks wisdom [to guide him through a decision or circumstance], he is to ask of [our benevolent] God, who gives to everyone generously and without rebuke or blame, and it will be given to him. **-James 1:5(AMP)**

Our God is all-knowing. He has complete and unlimited knowledge about everyone's situation. Guess what... He willing to give you the insight and strategy you need to be successful! Ask God for wisdom! You have access, just ask in faith!

Personal Reflection and Application:

_____
_____
_____
_____
_____
_____
_____
_____
_____
_____

Weekend 27

Let Me Love You

And now there remain: Faith [abiding trust in God and His promises], hope [confident expectation of eternal salvation], love [unselfish love for others growing out of God's love for me], these three [the choicest graces]; but the greatest of these is love. **-1 Corinthians 13:13 (AMP)**

Most of our lives we are taught to give love or walk in love. However, one of the greatest challenges for many people comes in the form of receiving it. Give others an opportunity to love you through your past hurts, offenses, and brokenness. Time does not heal all wounds. But love does!

Contributor- Shanita L. Rogers, Author, Public Speaker & Moderator

HEART

Friday

Date: _____

You have ravished my heart,
My sister, *my* spouse;
You have ravished my heart
With one *look* of your eyes
With one link of your necklace.
-Song of Solomon 4:9 (NKJV)

My darling, my bride, you excite me! You have stolen my heart with just one quick look from your eyes, with just one of the jewels from your necklace. **-Song of Solomon 4:9 (ERV)**

Marriage is beautiful and ordained by God. For the single ladies that desire to marry, I pray that God will bless you with a phenomenal husband who is excited to look upon and love you! For the married ladies, I pray that the fire continues to glow between the two of you and you continue to ravish his heart!

Personal Reflection and Application:

_____
_____
_____
_____
_____
_____
_____
_____
_____
_____
_____

GOD SPEAKS

Saturday

Date: _____

And the disciples came and said to Him, "Why do You speak to them in parables?" He answered and said to them, "Because it has been given to you to know the mysteries of the kingdom of heaven, but to them it has not been given." **-Matthew 13:10-11 (NKJV)**

Yes, He is speaking to you! God may not respond to your prayers the way that you are expecting, but He is responding. When the disciples asked Jesus why He was speaking in parables it was almost as if they were asking Him - why didn't He just speak in 'plain language.' In other words, why doesn't Jesus just give me His exact response directly – cut and dry. Well, sometimes He does but not always. It's important that you spend time listening to the Lord, so you will understand HOW He is speaking to you and WHAT He is saying!

Personal Reflection and Application:

_____
_____
_____
_____
_____
_____
_____
_____
_____
_____
_____

HOPE

Sunday

Date: _____

Against all hope, Abraham in hope believed and so became the father of many nations, just as it had been said to him, "So shall your offspring be."
-Romans 4:18 (NIV)

Sometimes you have to "hope against hope." When the situation is discouraging and the odds seem to be against you, don't give up! I think about the scripture that faith is the substance of things *hoped for*, so you need hope to build your faith. It's a choice to keep your hope despite any delay or denial. I choose to stay in a place of hope, and you can see it in my actions. I'm still striving and smiling – confident that like Abraham, God's promises shall come to pass in my life.

Personal Reflection and Application:

_____
_____
_____
_____
_____
_____
_____
_____
_____
_____
_____

Weekend 28

The Power of No

"But I discipline my body and bring it into subjection, lest, when
I have preached to others, I myself should become disqualified."

-1 Corinthians 9:27 (NKJV)

No one likes to be told No. I clearly remember the first time my natural
father told me no, I thought my world was ending (I was such a dramatic
child!). No sounds so negative and it is, or is it? Some good things can
come from a No, for example protection, peace, and growth. You know
that old saying, "you are what you eat?" Well, the same thing applies to
your flesh (spiritually and physically). You can't feed your flesh junk and
expect it to not be filled with and desire junk. But here's the thing about
our flesh, it wants what it wants, when it wants it and it hates the word
no! That is why we must make a daily decision to keep our flesh under
subjection. Putting your flesh under subjection requires being able to tell
your flesh, NO! The power to tell your flesh no to junk lies in our
connection to the power source, which is the Holy Spirit. He enables us
to live holy, He helps us keep our flesh under subjection, and He gives us
the power to say No. In 1 Corinthians 9: 27, Paul encourages us to bring
our flesh into subjection and he tells us why. It is so we, as believers don't
become disqualified from the race we are already set to win. Yes, it's a
"fixed" race, but you can disqualify yourself simply by not keeping your
flesh under subjection and not learning the Power of No.

Contributor- Bry-Anne E. Jones, MSW, LCSW

PRAY CONTINUALLY

Friday

Date: _____

pray continually
-1 Thessalonians 5:17 (NIV)

Never Stop Praying.
-1 Thessalonians 5:17 (NLT)

This may sound like a daunting task! How many times a day do we talk to our spouse, children, family member, colleagues or best girlfriend? Exactly, we need to commune more with the Lord! We may think, "I have STUFF to do and have limited prayer time." Well, think about the fact that God is omnipresent. Anytime and anywhere – He's available! Let's be fervent and intentional about prayer!

Personal Reflection and Application:

_____

_____

_____

_____

_____

_____

_____

_____

_____

_____

LOVE

Saturday

Date: _____

The first three words of **1 Corinthians 13:8**: Love never fails. **(NKJV)**

God's love outlasts every situation and circumstance. There is nothing we have ever done or failed to do for which God will not forgive us. Despite our imperfections, we never have to worry about losing God's love. His love endures forever. Be thankful for His Love!

Personal Reflection and Application:

_____

_____

_____

_____

_____

_____

_____

_____

_____

_____

_____

SPIRIT

Sunday

Date: _____

Now it happened, as we went to prayer, that a certain slave girl possessed with a spirit of divination met us, who brought her masters much profit by fortune-telling. This girl followed Paul and us, and cried out, saying, "These men are servants of the Most High God, who proclaim to us the way of salvation." And this she did for many days. But Paul, greatly annoyed, turned and said to the spirit, "I command you in the name of Jesus Christ to come out of her." And he came out that very hour. **-Acts 16:17-19 (NKJV)**

We can learn several lessons from this passage. The spiritual realm and unclean spirits are real. However, as a Christian, you can rest assured that your authority in the Name of Jesus is greater than any other spirit. I hear some people say that they are spiritual, and my question is—what spirit are you referencing? The devil always puts some truth in the situation to deceive people, so you must know your Word, have a personal relationship with the Lord and have other Christians around you to help recognize the tricks of the adversary. Remember, you have authority in Jesus' name!

Personal Reflection and Application:

_____
_____
_____
_____
_____
_____
_____
_____
_____
_____

Weekend 29

The Lord is my shepherd; I have all that I need. He lets me rest in green meadows; he leads me beside peaceful streams. He renews my strength. He guides me along right paths, bringing honor to his name. Even when I walk through the darkest valley, I will not be afraid, for you are close beside me. Your rod and your staff protect and comfort me. You prepare a feast for me in the presence of my enemies. You honor me by anointing my head with oil. My cup overflows with blessings. Surely your goodness and unfailing love will pursue me all the days of my life, and I will live in the house of the Lord forever. **-Psalm 23 (NLT)**

The Lord ALWAYS leads and guides me.

Contributor- Barbara Wilson, Mother of Capresha Caldwell

DIVINE PROTECTION

Friday

Date: _____

See, I have set the land before you; go in and possess the land which the LORD swore to your fathers—to Abraham, Isaac, and Jacob—to give to them and their descendants after them.' **-Deuteronomy 1:8 16 (NKJV)**

Over the years, I have learned that the promises of God do not necessarily include a red carpet. You may encounter challenges and question your journey. Do not give up on the promises! Stay focused, be strategic and continue to move faith forward!

Personal Reflection and Application:

_____

_____

_____

_____

_____

_____

_____

_____

_____

_____

_____

HOLY

Saturday

Date: _____

Because it is written, Be ye holy: for I am holy. **-1 Peter 1:15 (KJV)**

We can't allow this cultural to desensitize us to sin. We must strive to live according to the Word of God and not the standard of this world. Our lives must be pleasing and acceptable in God's sight. Keep God first in your life and go from Glory to Glory!

Personal Reflection and Application:

_____
_____
_____
_____
_____
_____
_____
_____
_____
_____
_____

ON FIRE

Sunday

Date: _____

I know your works, that you are neither cold nor hot. I could wish you were cold or hot. So then, because you are lukewarm, and neither cold nor hot, I will vomit you out of My mouth. **-Revelations 3: 15-16**

The enemy and this society will try to dilute the Word of God. Do you remember when you first accepted Christ and how you were on fire for the things of God? Where is that fire now? God's Word didn't change – we did. We must stay aware and ensure that life doesn't cause us to lose the love and passion for the Lord and His Word!

Personal Reflection and Application:

_____
_____
_____
_____
_____
_____
_____
_____
_____
_____

Weekend 30

"And He was withdrawn from them about a stone's throw, and He knelt down and prayed, saying, "Father, if it is Your will, take this cup away from Me; nevertheless not My will, but Yours, be done." **-Luke 22: 41- 42**

One day, one of my prayer requests was not answered the way I wanted it to be answered (key word "I"), and I got frustrated. I yelled at God, "Why am I even asking, if You are just going to do what You want to do anyway?!" (I'm sure I sounded like a bratty, spoiled, entitled teenager). Don't worry, I quickly repented as I remembered that 1. God is sovereign 2. He is in control 3. He always has my best interest in mind, even when He says no and 4. His will is what I want. Jesus knew the magnitude of the task His Father sent Him to earth to complete. Right before He was going to be betrayed by one of the people closest to Him (which would set the final part of His Father's plan of redemption in motion), He went to His Father in prayer. He asked Him, "Father, if thou be willing, remove this cup from me." He prayed to the point in which "His sweat was as it were great drops of blood falling to the ground" (Luke 22:44 NKJV). This request highlights His humanity (I am positive He experienced every human emotion in that moment, even frustration). During those times in which we are frustrated or faced with challenges, and want the "cup" to be passed, our response must be like Jesus. "Nevertheless, not my will, but thine will be done." Nothing we face could ever compare to what Jesus faced, but He models how we can face challenges, tasks (especially those we don't want to do), and yes even our frustrations, and win. How you ask? By submitting our will unto God's. It is imperative that we keep a "Nevertheless" in our spirit. When we are frustrated that things did not go our way we find peace in knowing that it went His way.

Contributor- Bry-Anne E. Jones, MSW, LCSW

PREPARATION

Friday

Date: _____

She also rises while it is yet night, And provides food for her household, And a portion for her maidservants. -**Proverbs 31:15**

Success requires sacrifice and preparation! The Proverbs 31 woman seems to be the total package and has everything together, but it didn't just fall into place. In this passage, she sacrifices the comfort of sleeping late and puts forth the effort and forethought of preparation for her household and employees. When you see another woman that has accomplished what you're striving to achieve, you have to ask yourself a question. Are you willing to pay the price that she paid? For the woman that you want to become, are you willing to put forth the necessary effort? I encourage women to do the work, so they can fulfill their God-given goals. If you add to your faith work, and you will achieve success!

Personal Reflection and Application:

_____

_____

_____

_____

_____

_____

_____

_____

_____

Capresha Caldwell

HONESTY

Saturday

Date: _____

In her deep anguish Hannah prayed to the Lord, weeping bitterly. And she made a vow, saying, "Lord Almighty, if you will only look on your servant's misery and remember me, and not forget your servant but give her a son, then I will give him to the Lord for all days of his life, and no razor will ever be used on his head." **-1 Samuel 1:10-11 (NKJV)**

Hannah wanted a son more than anything else. She poured her heart out to God and told Him exactly what she was willing to do if He blessed her. There have been numerous times in my Christian walk where I have had 'honest' conversations with God. And let me tell you – I know they touched the heart of God, because He responded and met me at my point of need. Have an honest conversation with the Lord!

Personal Reflection and Application:

_____
_____
_____
_____
_____
_____
_____
_____
_____
_____
_____

125

PEACE

Sunday

Date: _____

Stand therefore, having girded your waist with truth, having put on the breastplate of righteousness, and having shod your feet with the preparation of the gospel of peace; **-Ephesians 6:14-15 (NKJV)**

Before you put on your Tiffany's, pearls, business suit, uniform or any article of clothing – put on TRUTH, RIGHTEOUSNESS AND PEACE. Your greatest assignment is to ultimately represent the Kingdom of God to the world, so properly prepare yourself in the morning.

➤ Jesus is the TRUTH **(John 14:6)**
➤ You are RIGHTEOUS before God through faith in Jesus **(Romans 3:22)**
➤ Jesus is the Prince of PEACE **(Isaiah 9:6)**

Personal Reflection and Application:

_____
_____
_____
_____
_____
_____
_____
_____
_____
_____
_____

Weekend 31

A Change of Heart

Be kind and helpful to one another, tenderhearted [compassionate, understand], forgiving one another [readily and freely], just as God in Christ also forgave you. **-Ephesians 4:32 (AMP)**

When you are challenged with forgiving someone who has hurt you remember the process is more about you than it is the other person. Most importantly your responsibility is to honor God through your obedience. So when you desire to forgive but feel some resistance confess before God that you forgive the person who has hurt or offended you. Your words have the ability to change your heart.

Contributor- Shanita L. Rogers, Author, Public Speaker & Moderator

PRAYER

Friday

Date: _____

But when you pray, go into your room, close the door and pray to your Father, who is unseen. Then your Father, who sees what is done in secret, will reward you. **-Matthew 6:6 (NIV)**

We all need to be reminded that prayer is a foundational part of our Christian walk. It sustains us through the seasons of life because it's our bridge to stay connected to the Lord. You must be intentional with your prayer life! On purpose, take time and pull away from the distractions of life. I keep a fairly busy schedule, so I'm totally sympathetic to busy people. However, this is not an option but rather a necessity to maintaining a healthy Christian walk with the Lord. The rewards are two-fold because you get to bathe in the presence of the Lord and receive His blessings.

Personal Reflection and Application:

_____
_____
_____
_____
_____
_____
_____
_____
_____
_____

HEART CHECK

Saturday

Date: _____

Now hope does not disappoint, because the love of God has been poured out in our hearts by the Holy Spirit who was given to us. **-Romans 5:5 (NKJV)**

By the Holy Spirit, we have the love of God in our hearts. What's in our hearts dictates our actions and words. It's important that our actions and treatment of others reflect the love of God in our hearts. In all situations, we must stop and ask—what's in my heart?

Personal Reflection and Application:

_____

_____

_____

_____

_____

_____

_____

_____

_____

_____

_____

HEALING

Sunday

Date: _____

He sent them an assuring word and healed them: He rescued them from the pits where they were trapped. **-Psalm 107:20 NET**

God's Word provides us with healing. But don't limit the healing to just your physical body. His Word provides healing for your relationships, finances, emotions, and every aspect of your life. You don't have to live with brokenness. Instead, receive the healing power of God's Word!

Personal Reflection and Application:

_____
_____
_____
_____
_____
_____
_____
_____
_____
_____
_____

Weekend 32

Your Creator is Your Husband

For your Creator will be your husband; the Lord of Heaven's Armies is His name! He is your Redeemer, the Holy One of Israel, the God of all the earth. **-Isaiah 54:5 (NLT)**

God cares about the small things in our daily lives! I was having an issue with the neighbor's trash and with my vehicle. I was thinking that if I was married, my husband could handle these issues. Then I remembered that God is my Husband! I talked to the Lord about it and I no longer have an issue with my neighbor's trash and my car is fine. I have seen God's faithfulness like this before.

Several years ago, I was living in Maryland and purchased a big screen TV. When I got home, I was unable to lift it out of my car and had no one to help. As I stood in the parking lot, I asked, "Lord, until my husband comes, will You send someone to help me?"

A gentleman that lived in that neighborhood walked up and offered to help me. He picked it up out of the vehicle, put it on a cart and rolled to the front door of my secured building. He refused to allow me to pay him. I rolled it into my building and used the elevator to easily get it to my apartment. Even when I get married, God will still be my husband because He is my source!

PATIENCE

Friday

Date: _____

Love is patient… **-1 Corinthians 13:4 (NIV)**

We are not perfect, so I am thankful that God is patient. Continue striving for perfection, knowing that God is patiently guiding you through the process. Show people God's love today by being patient with them. **His patience is perfecting you!**

Personal Reflection and Application:

_____

_____

_____

_____

_____

_____

_____

_____

_____

_____

GOD'S SUPPORT

Saturday

Date: _____

May our Lord Jesus Christ himself and God our Father, who loved us and by his grace gave us eternal encouragement and good hope, encourage your hearts and strengthen you in every good deed and word. **-2 Thessalonians 2:16–17 (NIV)**

What goals, visions, and desires has God placed in your heart? Don't be overwhelmed or discouraged—receive God's encouragement, and let your heart be strengthened today! Go forth in your calling in God! You have His support!

Personal Reflection and Application:

_____

_____

_____

_____

_____

_____

_____

_____

_____

_____

_____

_____

LOVE HIS WORD

Sunday

Date: _____

Your word is very pure; Therefore Your servant loves it. **-Psalm 119:140 (NKJV)**

I love your word. Time and again it has been proven true. **-Psalm 119:140 (ERV)**

Reading and studying the Word of God should not be a chore. Yes, it does require time, energy, and effort, but it should be a labor of love. We make time to do the things that we want and love to do.

Personal Reflection and Application:

_____
_____
_____
_____
_____
_____
_____
_____
_____
_____

Weekend 33

Sleep

When you lie down, you will not be afraid; Yes, you will lie down and your sleep will be sweet. **-Proverbs 3:24 (NKJV)**

Despite the day or even the week that you had, do not allow the stress of life to keep you up at night worrying and restless. Cast your cares upon the Lord and ask for His wisdom. Proper sleep is essential to a quality life and healthy body. Take refuge and comfort in the Lord and enjoy sweet sleep!

ADORNED IN THE WORD

Friday

Date: _____

Therefore I love Your commandments More than gold, yes, than fine gold! **-Psalm 119:127 (NKJV)**

I have heard that diamonds are a girl's best friend. I know ladies get excited to see a Tiffany's box. But while we may enjoy nice jewelry, our love for the Word must be greater! Jewelry allows us to decorate the outside, but the Word purifies and sustains us from the inside out. That Word looks good on you!

Personal Reflection and Application:

_____
_____
_____
_____
_____
_____
_____
_____
_____
_____
_____

Capresha Caldwell

PEACE IN THE WORD

Saturday

Date: _____

Great peace have those who love Your law, and nothing causes them to stumble. **-Psalm 119:165 (NKJV)**

No matter the situation, you can find peace in His Word. No matter the circumstance or challenge, you can find victory in His Word. As ladies, sometimes we say how we love shoes, purses and make-up. But can we say that we love the word of God? To love the word of God, we must recognize how precious and powerful it is. Set your heart on God's Word!

Personal Reflection and Application:

_____
_____
_____
_____
_____
_____
_____
_____
_____
_____
_____

VICTORY IN THE WORD

Sunday

Date: _____

Yet in all these things we are more than conquerors through Him who loved us. **-Romans 8:37 (NKJV)**

As you end this weekend, and prepare for the new week, make the decision to enter your new week proclaiming you are more than a conqueror over every challenge! Choose to believe God's report! You are more than a conqueror in your health, finances, personal relationships, businesses and career!

Personal Reflection and Application:

_____
_____
_____
_____
_____
_____
_____
_____
_____
_____
_____

Weekend 34

Making the Right Decisions

Beloved, I pray that you may prosper in all things and be in health, just as your soul prospers. **-3 John 1:2 (NKJV)**

In order to prosper and experience good health, we must make right decisions. In most cases, it takes more than one right decision to change our circumstances. Making decisions daily to exercise and eat right can produce a healthy body. Deciding to save and invest our money versus frivolous spending increases our bank accounts. Choosing to be patient, kind and forgiving towards friends and family yields blessed relationships. God wants us to experience life, so we must align ourselves with Him by making right decisions!

LOVE AND HOSPITALITY

Friday

Date: _____

As Jesus and his disciples were on their way, he came to a village where a woman named Martha opened her home to him. She had a sister called Mary, who sat at the Lord's feet listening to what he said. **-Luke 10:38-39 (NIV)**

Martha showed love and hospitality by welcoming Jesus into her home. The Lord does not force Himself into our lives, but He gladly accepts the invitation. Invite the Lord into your home. Remember what you do to the least, you do unto Jesus (Matthew 25:40) Purpose in your heart to show 'hospitality' to people in need this year. It's not about necessarily inviting them to your home but rather reaching out to meet a need.

Personal Reflection and Application:

_____
_____
_____
_____
_____
_____
_____
_____
_____
_____
_____

PEACE

Saturday

Date: _____

Let the peace of Christ [the inner calm of one who walks daily with Him] be the controlling factor in your hearts [deciding and settling questions that arise]. **-Colossians 3:15 (AMP)**

As you are seeking the direction of the Lord, follow His peace. In some situations, God may give you a specific word of direction. If you don't have a specific word, follow God's peace. For instance, the Lord never *told* me to attend law school in Tennessee. As I prayed and walked by faith, I had His peace. When I moved to Maryland after law school, I did not have a specific word from the Lord. I stepped out in faith and followed His peace. When I returned to North Carolina from Maryland, I had both a specific word and His peace. Remember that the Lord has made His peace available to you.

Personal Reflection and Application:

_____
_____
_____
_____
_____
_____
_____
_____
_____
_____
_____

HOPE

Sunday

Date: _____

I remain confident of this: I will see the goodness of the LORD in the land of the living. **-Psalm 27:13 (NIV)**

Stay hopeful! There is still plenty of time to receive God's blessings for you and your family! Continue to have great expectations, knowing that God has marvelous things in store for you this year and years to come!

Personal Reflection and Application:

_____
_____
_____
_____
_____
_____
_____
_____
_____
_____

Weekend 35

Travel Light

If a man therefore purge himself from these, he shall be a vessel unto honour, sanctified, and meet for the master's use, and prepared unto every good work. -2 **Timothy 2:21 KJV**

I recently went on an international trip with my family. As a crew of five, we were able to condense our luggage to just three bags among us. Everyone's bag was the required weight but mine. As you can imagine, I was trying to compromise between what I needed and what I wanted. Much is the same in our lives - deciding between needs and wants. Daily we have to decide what we will carry on life's journey.

You have a good work to do so fill your luggage or vessel with good things that God can use like kindness, grace, love and faith. And eliminate fear, doubt, hate and anger. Travel light my sister!

Contributor- Roshanda "The Rosho" Pratt, First Lady of Visibility

GRACE

Friday

Date: _____

For the law was given through Moses, *but* grace and truth came through Jesus Christ. **-John 1:17 (NKJV)**

NEWS FLASH—you do not have to be perfect! You do not have to fulfill the law. The Lord is not condemning you, so don't condemn yourself. Open your heart to Jesus and receive GRACE.

Personal Reflection and Application:

_____
_____
_____
_____
_____
_____
_____
_____
_____
_____

PRAISE

Saturday

Date: _____

About midnight Paul and Silas were praying and singing hymns to God, and the other prisoners were listening to them. Suddenly there was such a violent earthquake that the foundations of the prison were shaken. At once all the prison doors flew open, and everyone's chains came loose.
-Acts 16:25–26 (NIV)

Even in your most challenging times (any form of darkness and bondage), never stop praising and trusting God. He can and will deliver you SUDDENLY!

Personal Reflection and Application:

_____
_____
_____
_____
_____
_____
_____
_____
_____
_____
_____

VICTORY

Sunday

Date: _____

And he said, "Listen, all you of Judah and you inhabitants of Jerusalem, and you, King Jehoshaphat! Thus says the LORD to you: 'Do not be afraid nor dismayed because of this great multitude, for the battle *is* not yours, but God's. Tomorrow go down against them. They will surely come up by the Ascent of Ziz, and you will find them at the end of the brook before the Wilderness of Jeruel. You will not *need* to fight in this *battle*. Position yourselves, stand still and see the salvation of the LORD, who is with you, O Judah and Jerusalem!' Do not fear or be dismayed; tomorrow go out against them, for the LORD *is* with you. **-2 Chronicles 20:15-17 (NKJV)**

Jehoshaphat knew he could not win the battle alone. He put his faith in God! You are not facing your 'battles' alone. Trust God for the Victory!

Personal Reflection and Application:

_____
_____
_____
_____
_____
_____
_____
_____
_____
_____

Weekend 36

All Is Well

So he said, "Why are you going to him today? *It is* neither the New Moon nor the Sabbath. And she said, "*It is* well." Then she saddled a donkey, and said to her servant, "Drive, and go forward; do not slacken the pace for me unless I tell you." And so she departed, and went to the man of God at Mount Carmel. So it was, when the man of God saw her afar off, that he said to his servant Gehazi, "Look, the Shunammite woman! Please run now to meet her, and say to her, '*Is it* well with you? *Is it* well with your husband? *Is it* well with the child?' " And she answered, "*It is* well." **-2 Kings 4:23-26 (NKJV)**

Notice how she said, "It is well," several times. Keep in mind that she only desired one thing from the Lord, a son. God blessed her with a son, but he just died in her lap. Instead of her getting all emotional and falling apart, she positioned herself in a stance of faith. Despite her son's death, she spoke words of faith over the situation that 'all was well.' Through your words, you can curse or bless your life! Then she traveled to see the man of God, Elisha. She added the appropriate corresponding action. This woman added works to her faith. The end result – her son was raised from the dead.

As I reflect on my life, I can't ignore the bad, but I have to celebrate the good. I see certain areas of my life where I have been fruitful and others where I have been barren. I am positioning myself to receive all of the God-given desires of my heart. I decree that ALL IS WELL!

FRUITFUL

Friday

Date: _____

But the fruit of the Spirit [the result of His presence within us] is love [unselfish concern for others], joy, [inner] peace, patience [not the ability to wait, but how we act while waiting], kindness, goodness, faithfulness, gentleness, self-control. Against such things there is no law.
-Galatians 5: 22-23 (AMP)

The best fruit that we can bear in our lives is to show others the character of God. To have a fruitful life that's a blessing to others, we must yield and cooperate with the Spirit of God.

Personal Reflection and Application:

_____
_____
_____
_____
_____
_____
_____
_____
_____
_____

Caldwell

GRACE

Saturday

Date: _____

The grace of our Lord Jesus Christ *be* with you all. Amen. **-Romans 16:24 (NKJV)**

One night, we had an awesome Bible Study focusing on the Grace of God. I am presenting you with the same challenge from that session. Look at yourself—recognize and acknowledge the grace of God in and on your life!

Personal Reflection and Application:

_____
_____
_____
_____
_____
_____
_____
_____
_____
_____
_____

LAUGHTER

Sunday

Date: _____

A merry heart does good, like medicine, but a broken spirit dries the bones. -**Proverbs 17:22 (NKJV)**

Even though you are busy and have numerous responsibilities, your heavenly Father does not want you stressed out over life. Take time to smile and laugh on purpose! I am convinced that God has a sense of humor! Thank Him for your blessings and trust Him with your challenges. Smile and laugh on purpose today!

Personal Reflection and Application:

_____

_____

_____

_____

_____

_____

_____

_____

_____

_____

Weekend 37

All Things Are Possible

Jesus looked at them and said, "With man this is impossible, but with God all things are possible." **-Matthew 9:23 (NIV)**

I pray that you are well and encouraged! As many of you know, I want to own an ice cream shop and I am praying for the provisions to launch it. The other day I went to an ice cream shop down the street from my home. There was an African American woman working and it turns out that she and her husband are the owners! I asked her why she started the shop. She replied that God led them to start the business. I smiled with glee – what?! I asked her about funding. She explained that the bank wasn't willing to give them a loan for the opening, but they knew it was God's direction, so they looked at their resources and were able to afford starting the business. This experience encouraged me to know that with the help of God, I can have my dream of owning an ice cream shop! What looks impossible in your life? Trust and know that with God it is possible!

FAITH

Friday

Date: _____

And the Lord answered, If you had faith (trust and confidence in God) even [so small] like a grain of mustard seed, you could say to this mulberry tree, Be pulled up by the roots, and be planted in the sea, and it would obey you. **-Luke 17:6 (AMP)**

Let's do a comparison to gain greater insight into this scripture. A mustard seed is about 1–2 mm in diameter and looks like a tiny grain in your hand. Depending on the type of mulberry tree, it can grow from 30–80 feet in height. What you may consider as small faith can get big results! Speaking in faith can cause a situation to be completely uprooted and moved out of your way. Faith speaks and gets results!

Personal Reflection and Application:

_____

_____

_____

_____

_____

_____

_____

_____

_____

_____

CONNECTED TO THE VINE

Saturday

Date: _____

I am the vine, and you are the branches. If you stay joined to me, and I to you, you will produce plenty of fruit. But separated from me you won't be able to do anything. **-John 15:5 (ERV)**

Recently, I was feeling overwhelmed by all of the "projects" in my life. How would I have enough time and energy to do everything?! The Lord reminded me that we are in this together. As long you stay connected to Him through prayer and time in the Word, you can accomplish everything!

Personal Reflection and Application:

_____

_____

_____

_____

_____

_____

_____

_____

_____

_____

_____

AGREE WITH THE WORD

Sunday

Date: _____

Do two walk together unless they have agreed to do so? **-Amos 3:3 (NIV)**

Ever felt like it's you against the world and you have to walk this journey alone? You are not alone! Continue on your life's journey with the Lord. He is leading you to a place of peace, victory, health, abundance, beauty, and joy. Agree with His word and walk in His way!

Personal Reflection and Application:

_____
_____
_____
_____
_____
_____
_____
_____
_____
_____
_____

Weekend 38

Rising Early to Pray

Now in the morning, having risen a long while before daylight, He went out and departed to a solitary place; and there He prayed. **-Mark 1:35 (NKJV)**

This scripture is about Jesus rising early to pray. One morning, the Holy Spirit woke me up between 3 – 4 am, so I began praying. I had a situation that day and was so grateful that the Lord prepped me for it. It's so important that we follow Jesus and start our day off with prayer. It takes discipline to get out of bed early but it's so worth it. I like having a designated place to fellowship. I can leave my Bible and journal in that spot. When I arrive to that area, it's like my meeting place to sit and commune with God. In that place and time, we can focus on Him, receive His direction and be reminded of His love for us.

PEACE

Friday

Date: _____

And let the peace (soul harmony which comes) from Christ rule (act as umpire continually) in your hearts [deciding and settling with finality all questions that arise in your minds, in that peaceful state] to which as [members of Christ's] one body you were also called [to live]. And be thankful (appreciative), [giving praise to God always]. -**Colossians 3:15 (AMP)**

Do you need a road map to navigate through the journey of life? You can relax and follow the peace of God. Let God's peace be your GPS!

Personal Reflection and Application:

_____

_____

_____

_____

_____

_____

_____

_____

_____

_____

_____

BLESSINGS

Saturday

Date: _____

"Glory to God in the highest, and on earth peace, goodwill toward men!"
-Luke 2:14 (NKJV)

Take time to reflect on the blessings that God has bestowed upon you. Take time to appreciate those that have made a difference in your life. Everything may not be perfect, but don't forget to count your blessings anyway! Thank God!

Personal Reflection and Application:

_____
_____
_____
_____
_____
_____
_____
_____
_____
_____

LOVE

Sunday

Date: _____

Whoever does not love does not know God, because God is love. **-1 John 4:8 (NIV)**

Situations, circumstances, jobs, people, finances, physical body...all may continue to change. One thing has remained constant—God's LOVE for you! In your time of reflection on the past and preparation for the future, remember...God is Love!

Personal Reflection and Application:

_____

_____

_____

_____

_____

_____

_____

_____

_____

_____

_____

Weekend 39

Feet Like Hinds' Feet

He makes my **feet** like **hinds' feet** [able to stand firmly and tread safely on paths of testing and trouble]; He sets me [securely] upon my high places. **-Psalm 18:33 (AMP)**

The Lord GOD is my strength [my source of courage, my invincible army]; He has made my **feet** [steady and sure] like **hinds' feet** and makes me walk [forward with spiritual confidence] on my high places [of challenge and responsibility]. **-Habakkuk 3:19 (AMP)**

Recently, I was at work and started to feel overwhelmed. Outside of work, I have a huge project that I'm working on in addition to an already busy lifestyle. Oh and life still happens – I needed new brakes and my laptop is acting crazy. In response, I literally started to feel nauseous. It's crazy to see how your mind and body handles stress. Today, I am reminded that I have the victory. God knows everything that I'm facing! I'm praying my way through – one step at a time. I think about one of my favorite books *Hinds Feet On High Places* by Hannah Hurnard. God gives us the strength and ability to go to new heights in Him. Stay encouraged and keep moving forward! We have the VICTORY!

MIND

Friday

Date: _____

Keep this Book of the Law always on your lips; meditate on it day and night, so that you may be careful to do everything written in it. Then you will be prosperous and successful. **-Joshua 1:8 (NIV); See also Psalm 1:1-3**

Meditating on the Word of God is the opposite of worrying about a problem. When you ponder on the Word of God, you will have peace, revelation, and direction. Worry causes stress and frustration. Focus on the Word and you shall experience great prosperity and success!

Personal Reflection and Application:

_____

_____

_____

_____

_____

_____

_____

_____

_____

_____

LIFE

Saturday

Date: _____

I call heaven and earth as witnesses against you today, that I have set before you life and death, the blessing and the curse; therefore, you shall choose life in order that you may live, you and your descendants.
-Deuteronomy 30:19 (AMP)

You have to make a decision… choose life! When you choose to forgive, to love, to laugh, to be optimistic, to exercise, to eat right, to count your blessings, to smile, to pray, to praise… you are choosing life! Most of all, when you choose to accept Jesus as your Lord and Savior, you are choosing life!

Personal Reflection and Application:

_____
_____
_____
_____
_____
_____
_____
_____
_____
_____
_____

DIVINE PROTECTION

Sunday

Date: _____

Because you have made the Lord, *who is* my refuge, *even* the Most High, your dwelling place, no evil shall befall you, nor shall any plague come near your dwelling; for He shall give His angels charge over you, to keep you in all your ways. In *their* hands they shall bear you up, lest you dash your foot against a stone. **-Psalm 91:9-12 (NKJV)**

Let's continue focusing on Psalm 91. For divine protection, you must dwell and stay in the will and presence of the Lord. I remember hearing a song with the lyric *the safest place is in the will of God.* Angels are real and assigned to protect! The Word of God includes numerous scriptures about angelic beings. Years ago, I was blessed to even see an angel. It was an awesome experience and I'm thankful for it!

Personal Reflection and Application:

_____
_____
_____
_____
_____
_____
_____
_____
_____
_____

Weekend 40

Do Not Be Deceived

Now the serpent was more crafty than any of the wild animals the Lord God had made. He said to the woman, "Did God really say, 'You must not eat from any tree in the garden'?" The woman said to the serpent, "We may eat fruit from the trees in the garden, but God did say, 'You must not eat fruit from the tree that is in the middle of the garden, and you must not touch it, or you will die.'" "You will not certainly die," the serpent said to the woman. "For God knows that when you eat from it your eyes will be opened, and you will be like God, knowing good and evil."

v.13 Then the Lord God said to the woman, "What is this you have done?" The woman said, "The serpent deceived me, and I ate." -**Genesis 3:1-5, 13 (NIV)**

Warning

The enemy will try to deceive you by attacking your mind and making you doubt what God said. I experienced this battle! He may start with a simply seed of doubt, "Did God really say?" Then he boldly contradicts God, "You will not certainly die." Deception produces wrong thoughts and leads to wrong actions! Believe God's Word over the lies of the enemy!

DIVINE PROTECTION

Friday

Date: _____

A wise man will hear and increase learning, and a man of understanding will attain wise counsel, To understand a proverb and an enigma, The words of the wise and their riddles. **-Proverbs 1:5-6 (NKJV)**

Two important keys to walking in wisdom. Connect with the right people that can provide you with sound counsel. Stay open to learning, growing and maturing. As I am embarking on a new area that the Lord is leading me to, I am developing on purpose! I am seeking the guidance of seasoned mentors and attending training.

You are a wise woman, so make the right connections and stay teachable! God has already put awesomeness in you! It's time for those gifts that God has put in you to come forth!

Personal Reflection and Application:

_____

_____

_____

_____

_____

_____

_____

_____

_____

_____

Capresha Caldwell

FAITH

Saturday

Date: _____

"'If you can'?" said Jesus. "Everything is possible for one who believes."
-Mark 9:23 (NIV)

Set your focus and your faith on God's Word. Believe God's Word and see the manifestation of His promises. Faith and works equal results!

Personal Reflection and Application:

_____
_____
_____
_____
_____
_____
_____
_____
_____
_____
_____

YOU'RE NEVER ALONE

Sunday

Date: _____

I can do all things through Christ who strengthens me. **-Philippians 4:13 (NKJV)**

ALL things—you do not have to deal with situations alone! He is with you and will strengthen you. Your strength may run out, but His supply is unlimited! Stay the Course!

Personal Reflection and Application:

_____

_____

_____

_____

_____

_____

_____

_____

_____

_____

Weekend 41

Speak Life!

Death and life are in the power of the tongue, And those who love it *and* indulge it will eat its fruit *and* bear the consequences of their words. **-Proverbs 18:21 (AMP)**

I shall speak Life into and over my Life for the rest of my Life! -Marvin Sapp

LOVE CONFRONTS SIN

Friday

Date: _____

But you, beloved, build yourselves up on [the foundation of] your most holy faith [continually progress, rise like an edifice higher and higher], pray in the Holy Spirit, and keep yourselves in the love of God, waiting anxiously *and* looking forward to the mercy of our Lord Jesus Christ [which will bring you] to eternal life. And have mercy on some, who are doubting; save others, snatching them out of the fire; and on some have mercy but with fear, loathing even the clothing spotted *and* polluted by their shameless immoral freedom. **-Jude 1:20-23 (AMP)**

I attended a Joyce Meyers Conference. One comment from her that sticks with me is "Love confronts Sin." During the conference, she talked about the importance of helping Christians (not unbelievers) stay out of sin. We must ensure that the Bible is our standard. This message made me evaluate my life and it stirred up my zeal to help those around me walk out a life of obedience to God. Praying in the Spirit puts us in a position to hear from God about corrections in our lives and to help others on their Christian walk.

Personal Reflection and Application:

_____
_____
_____
_____
_____
_____
_____
_____
_____
_____

COUNSEL

Saturday

Date: _____

Where there is no counsel, purposes are frustrated, but with many counselors they are accomplished. **-Proverbs 15:22 (AMP)**

The other day I was thinking about my different career and business options. I was truly racking my brain about the timeline and direction I should go. I was talking to the Lord about guidance. Then I remembered that God has put some awesome people in my life. I have people that I can consult with and gain some valuable nuggets. I don't have to sit around pondering alone. Take time to recognize the resources that God has placed in your life!

Personal Reflection and Application:

_____
_____
_____
_____
_____
_____
_____
_____
_____
_____
_____

REST

Sunday

Date: _____

Six days you shall work, but on the seventh day you shall rest; in plowing time and in harvest you shall rest. **-Exodus 34:21 (NKJV)**

I've been pretty busy lately and knew that I needed to slow down and get some rest. When I came home one day, my body let me know that it was at its limit. I was just grateful to make it to my sofa. I'm resting, organizing my schedule and setting up systems to ensure that I can complete tasks and still have time to rest. Are you resting?

Personal Reflection and Application:

_____

_____

_____

_____

_____

_____

_____

_____

_____

_____

_____

Weekend 42

His Appointed Time

And the Lord visited Sarah as He had said, and the Lord did for Sarah as He had spoken. For Sarah conceived and bore Abraham a son in his old age, *at the set time of which God had spoken to him.* **Genesis 21:1-2(NKJV)** (Italics added)

Sarah received her blessing within God's timing and not man's timing. She was pass childbearing age, but God had an ordained time for her, and He is greater than any natural law. Don't compare your life to others and their blessings. Just trust God that you shall have everything that He has promised in His appointed time.

LOVE

Friday

Date: _____

For God so loved the world that he gave his one and only Son, that whoever believes in him shall not perish but have eternal life. **-John 3:16 (NIV)**

Before you were born, God loved you and was thinking about you! Guess what—you are still on His mind and in His heart! Out of His love for you...He gave Jesus! Receive Christ—He's the only solution to every problem!

Personal Reflection and Application:

_____

_____

_____

_____

_____

_____

_____

_____

_____

_____

_____

Capresha Caldwell

PATIENCE

Saturday

Date: _____

...through faith and patience inherit what has been promised. **-Hebrews 6:12b (NIV)**

Have you ever traveled with children? As soon as you pull out of the driveway, the kids ask, "Are we there yet?" Just a few miles down the street and again they ask, "Are we there yet?!" Sometimes we are like those children. We believe God to fulfill His promises, but we are tired of waiting! God knows the destination, the route, the detours, and the expected time of arrival. Patiently believe and receive!

Personal Reflection and Application:

_____
_____
_____
_____
_____
_____
_____
_____
_____
_____
_____

REST

Sunday

Date: _____

Then it shall come to pass, because you listen to these judgments, and keep and do them, that the LORD your God will keep with you the covenant and the mercy which He swore to your fathers. And He will love you and bless you and multiply you; He will also bless the fruit of your womb and the fruit of your land, your grain and your new wine and your oil, the increase of your cattle and the offspring of your flock, in the land of which He swore to your fathers to give you. **-Deuteronomy 7:12-13 (NKJV)**

How do you have a fruitful and blessed life? Obedience! We have a covenant (an agreement) with God. Comply with the terms (obey) and receive the benefits!

Personal Reflection and Application:

_____
_____
_____
_____
_____
_____
_____
_____
_____
_____
_____

Weekend 43

A Plan of Restoration

Then the Lord God said to the woman, "What is this you have done?" The woman said, "The serpent deceived me, and I ate."
-Genesis 3:13 (NIV)

This week I was reflecting on some areas of my life and started wondering if I made a mistake and messed up some things that God had planned. Then I saw a post from a Facebook friend that said "If you think you've blown God's plan for your life, rest in this. You, my friend, are not that powerful." That message really encouraged my heart! Yes, Eve was deceived by the serpent and made a mistake. Then Adam made the same mistake, and they were kicked out of the Garden of Eden. However, God already had a plan of restoration thru Christ Jesus. For your shortcomings and mistakes, God already has a plan to restore you!

PUSH

Friday

Date: _____

I was pushed back and about to fall, but the LORD helped me. **-Psalm 118:13 (NIV)**

Don't allow challenging situations to bully you! The Lord Jesus has your back and will help you. Instead of being pushed by negative circumstances, you must push forward in faith!

He is greater than any setback! In **P**rayer, gain **U**nderstanding, **S**trength, and **H**ope!

Personal Reflection and Application:

_____
_____
_____
_____
_____
_____
_____
_____
_____
_____
_____

A FINISHED WORK

Saturday

Date: _____

...being confident of this, that he who began a good work in you will carry it on to completion until the day of Christ Jesus. **-Philippians 1:6 (NIV)**

And I am sure that God who began the good work within you will keep right on helping you grow in his grace until his task within you is finally finished on that day when Jesus Christ returns. **-Philippians 1:6 (TLB)**

God is doing a work in you, and it is good! Unlike some people, God completes whatever He starts. He has not and will not abandon you. Stay encouraged—He is not finished with you yet!

Personal Reflection and Application:

_____
_____
_____
_____
_____
_____
_____
_____
_____
_____
_____

ROOTED IN THE WORD

Sunday

Date: _____

That person is like a tree planted by streams of water, which yields its fruit in season and whose leaf does not wither— whatever they do prospers.
-Psalm 1:3 (NIV)

The challenges in life are opportunities for you to get rooted and grounded in God and His Word. Your root system in the Word of God will sustain you and will produce a fruitful, blessed life. Stay encouraged—you are breaking new ground!

Personal Reflection and Application:

_____
_____
_____
_____
_____
_____
_____
_____
_____
_____
_____

Weekend 44

Unique and Loved

Now Jesus loved Martha and her sister and Lazarus **-John 11:5(NKJV)**

My focus is to help people understand their 'uniqueness,' without the concern of someone else having a 'better' personality. We should never feel bad about how God has made us. Sure, we all need to obey God's Word but embrace your uniqueness. Mary and Martha were very different, but God loved them both. When Jesus came to their home, Mary sat at His feet while Martha started cooking. Don't compare yourself to others. God loves and accepts your 'uniqueness,' so You and the people in your life must do the same!

HOPE

Friday

Date: _____

Now faith is the substance of things hoped for, the evidence of things not seen. **-Hebrews 11:1 (NKJV)**

There is a connection between hope and faith. The scripture states that "faith is the substance of things hoped for..." Hope is a prerequisite to receiving the manifested blessings of God in your life. You must have hope—a great desire or expectancy for something, and then exercise your faith to receive the manifestation.

Personal Reflection and Application:

_____

_____

_____

_____

_____

_____

_____

_____

_____

_____

DIVINE PROTECTION

Saturday

Date: _____

"Because he has set his love upon Me, therefore I will deliver him; I will set him on high, because he has known My name. He shall call upon Me, and I will answer him; I *will be* with him in trouble; I will deliver him and honor him. With long life I will satisfy him, and show him My salvation."
-Psalm 91:14-16 (NKJV)

Thank God that He gives you a long life! In times of trouble, call on the Lord with confidence knowing that He answers and delivers you!

Personal Reflection and Application:

_____
_____
_____
_____
_____
_____
_____
_____
_____
_____
_____

FOCUSED

Sunday

Date: _____

Why, my soul, are you downcast? Why so disturbed within me? Put your hope in God, for I will yet praise him, my Savior and my God. **-Psalm 43:5 (NIV)**

Whenever you experience negative feelings, emotions, or thoughts, you do not have to let those feelings dominate you. Sometimes you have to talk to yourself instead! You must give voice to your faith!

Stay focused on the Word of God, and your heart will not be troubled. Encourage yourself in the lord!

Personal Reflection and Application:

_____
_____
_____
_____
_____
_____
_____
_____
_____
_____
_____

Weekend 45

Without Complaint

Do all things without complaining and disputing -**Philippians 2:14 (NKJV)**

At times, I have had a challenging time at work and admit that I have complained. Finally, I had to sit down in the office and repent. I told the Lord that I would stop complaining and trust Him. In turn, He gave me direction, and lifted the pressure. Trusting and praising God will lead you to the path of success!

FREE

Friday

Date: _____

Therefore, there is now no condemnation for those who are in Christ Jesus, because through Christ Jesus the law of the Spirit who gives life has set you free from the law of sin and death. **-Romans 8:1-2 (NIV)**

You are FREE in Christ Jesus. Do not allow any person, situation or even your own thoughts tell you otherwise. Christ is more than enough to cover your imperfections. Give thanks for the freedom that Christ has provided for you!

Personal Reflection and Application:

_____
_____
_____
_____
_____
_____
_____
_____
_____
_____

Caldwell

BLESSED

Saturday
Date: _____

I know how to be abased, and I know how to abound. Everywhere and in all things I have learned to be full and to be hungry, both to abound and to suffer need. I can do all things through Christ who strengthens me. **-Philippians 4:12-13 (NKJV)**

I always have a 'To-Do List' with goals to improve my life. Sometimes I'm so consumed with reaching my goals that I forget to appreciate my current situation. At times, the Lord reminds me to relax and count my blessings!

Personal Reflection and Application:

_____
_____
_____
_____
_____
_____
_____
_____
_____
_____
_____

185

VICTORY

Sunday

Date: _____

So he answered and said to me: "This is the word of the LORD to Zerubbabel: **'Not by might nor by power, but by My Spirit,'** Says the LORD of hosts. **-Zechariah 4:6 (NKJV, emphasis added)**

You are not expected to conquer challenges with your own strength! Let's face it—you need to rely on God. Instead of stressing and straining, you must have faith in God to bless you with the victory. Relax...He heard your prayer and is moving on your behalf!

Personal Reflection and Application:

_____
_____
_____
_____
_____
_____
_____
_____
_____
_____
_____

Weekend 46

A Woman of God

Give her of the fruit of her hands, And let her own works praise her in the gates. **-Proverbs 31: 10 – 31 (NKJV)**

I only quoted the last verse but please take time to read verses 10 – 31 of Proverbs 31. This passage represents a wise and virtuous woman, regardless of your marital status. The woman in Proverbs 31 was a businesswoman, she feared God, and she knew how to take care of her home and deal with people. I am reflecting on the progress that I have made and continue to make in my career, business, family, personal wellness and most importantly my Christian walk. And I realize something … God has put some good stuff in me! Don't count yourself short – take a moment to look at the awesomeness that God has placed in you. Thank Him and yield, so he can continue to develop you as an awesome and virtuous Woman of God.

SACRIFICE

Friday

Date: _____

Now Jesus sat opposite the treasury and saw how the people put money into the treasury. And many *who were* rich put in much. Then one poor widow came and threw in two mites, which make a quadrans. So He called His disciples to *Himself* and said to them, "Assuredly, I say to you that this poor widow has put in more than all those who have given to the treasury; for they all put in out of their abundance, but she out of her poverty put in all that she had, her whole livelihood." **-Mark 12: 41-44 (NKJV)**

It's not about people knowing our name. The focus is to set an example of Christ for others and to please the Lord. She imitated Christ by making a sacrifice and offering up everything she had. Her sacrificial actions pleased Him, and He took notice. She knew how to get Christ's attention! If you want to get His attention, open up and offer all you are and all you have to the Lord!

Personal Reflection and Application:

_____

_____

_____

_____

_____

_____

_____

_____

_____

_____

_____

GOD'S PLAN

Saturday

Date: _____

For I know the thoughts and plans that I have for you, says the Lord, thoughts and plans for welfare and peace and not for evil, to give you hope in your final outcome. **-Jeremiah 29:11 (AMP)**

Even when you find yourself on a "detour," God can guide you back to the main route. He has a good plan and knows the destination. We must rely on our God-Powered Solution

Personal Reflection and Application:

_____
_____
_____
_____
_____
_____
_____
_____
_____
_____
_____

FOR YOUR GOOD

Sunday

Date: _____

And we know that all things work together for good to those who love God, to those who are called according to His purpose. **-Romans 8:28 (NKJV)**

I made a wrong decision—a big "oops." When I realized the mistake that I had made and went to God in prayer, He lovingly reminded me that all things will still work together for my good. He assured me that He was still in control. God can handle your mistakes and turn them around for your good! We don't have to be perfect…He is!

Personal Reflection and Application:

_____
_____
_____
_____
_____
_____
_____
_____
_____
_____
_____

Weekend 47

Mother of All Living

And Adam called his wife's name Eve, because she was the mother of all living. **-Genesis 3:20 (NKJV)**

I had an opportunity to host an *In His Presence* Session at my Mother's home one day. Of course, all of the ladies that attended were mothers, aunts, and godmothers (I was the baby in the group). I love my elders and was honored by the opportunity to minister to them. As I looked at all of the women, I could only imagine the stories they could tell, the tears they have cried and the prayers that they have prayed for friends, family and even enemies. I could imagine how they have poured knowledge, wisdom and love into countless people. We play an important role in nurturing those that God has sent into our lives and across our paths. Mother's love when it's not convenient and even when it's not reciprocated. Recognize your role and the power of God's love within you to help someone else fulfill God's purpose in his or her life.

FORGIVENESS

Friday

Date: _____

Then the man said, "The woman whom You gave *to be* with me, she gave me of the tree, and I ate." **-Genesis 3:12 (NKJV)**

Adam was responsible for the Garden and Eve was taken out of the man (his rib to be more specific). Now as soon as something goes wrong in the Garden and God question's Adam, he points and squeals on Eve. Why didn't Adam just take the blame? I realized something – even though the people in our lives may truly love us, they may not always respond the way that we want them to respond. I wonder what Eve thought about his statement. When Adam and Eve got kicked out of the Garden, we don't see any scriptures about them arguing. As a matter of fact, in the very next chapter, Eve conceived a baby. Forgive the people in your life that truly love you but may not have handled a situation in the best manner.

Personal Reflection and Application:

_____
_____
_____
_____
_____
_____
_____
_____
_____
_____

PROMISE KEEPER

Saturday

Date: _____

God is not a man, that He should lie, Nor a son of man, that He should repent. Has he said, and will He not do? Or has He spoken, and will He not make it good? **-Numbers 23:19 (NKJV)**

You can trust God to fulfill His promises in your life. God loves you and would not lie to you. You know God is able, but sometimes you may wonder if He's willing. Yes, He is committed to "making good" on all of His promises in your life. God is your Promise Keeper!

Personal Reflection and Application:

_____

_____

_____

_____

_____

_____

_____

_____

_____

_____

_____

REST

Sunday

Date: _____

Come to Me, all you who labor and are heavy-laden and overburdened, and I will cause you to rest. [I will ease and relieve and refresh your souls.] Take My yoke upon you and learn of Me, for I am gentle (meek) and humble (lowly) in heart, and you will find rest (relief and ease and refreshment and recreation and blessed quiet) for your souls. For My yoke is wholesome (useful, good—not harsh, hard, sharp, or pressing, but comfortable, gracious, and pleasant), and My burden is light and easy to be borne. **-Matthew 11:28–30 (AMP)**

Do you need rest? God is inviting you to come and find rest in Him. Many times, we try to figure everything out on our own and become overwhelmed. God's way is the best way! If you follow His plan, then your soul can be refreshed. Lift your voice to the Lord today and ask Him to show you His plan and teach you how to walk in His way!

Personal Reflection and Application:

_____
_____
_____
_____
_____
_____
_____
_____
_____
_____
_____

Weekend 48

Don't Worry – God is in Control!

"Therefore I say to you, do not worry about your life, what you will eat or what you will drink; nor about your body, what you will put on. Is not life more than food and the body more than clothing?" -**Matthew 6:25 (NKJV)**

TRIUMPHANT

Friday

Date: _____

Now thanks be to God who always leads us in triumph in Christ, and through us diffuses the fragrance of His knowledge in every place. **-2 Corinthians 2:14 (NKJV)**

The truth of God's Word will change the reality of your situation. The situation may speak defeat, but God's Word speaks victory and triumph. Stay focused on God's word and confess the word daily. I agree with God! I am triumphant!

Personal Reflection and Application:

_____

_____

_____

_____

_____

_____

_____

_____

_____

_____

TRUST

Saturday
Date: _____

Lean on, trust in, and be confident in the Lord with all your heart and mind and do not rely on your own insight or understanding. - **Proverbs 3:5 (AMP)**

You may be accustomed to planning, organizing, and orchestrating everything in your life and in the lives of others. However, you must submit even those abilities and have confidence in the Lord to guide you through the unknown and the unseen. Trust in Him!

Personal Reflection and Application:

_____
_____
_____
_____
_____
_____
_____
_____
_____
_____

GUIDANCE

Sunday

Date: _____

In all your ways know, recognize, and acknowledge Him, and He will direct and make straight and plain your paths. **-Proverbs 3:6 (AMP)**

Whether you are facing a minuscule or colossal situation, seek God's direction. He is a good Father and cares about every aspect of your life. He will provide you with the guidance and direction that you need. Time to pray for guidance!

Personal Reflection and Application:

_____
_____
_____
_____
_____
_____
_____
_____
_____
_____
_____

Weekend 49

Faith for Generations

When I call to remembrance the genuine faith that is in you, which dwelt first in your grandmother Lois and you mother Eunice, and I am persuaded is in you also. **-2 Timothy 1:5 (NKJV)**

Paul is talking to his son in the Lord, Timothy. He takes note that both Timothy's grandmother and mother had great faith. It's wonderful to pass a natural inheritance but a spiritual inheritance is priceless. I really appreciate women that are seasoned in their walk with the Lord. They have such a powerful testimony of His faithfulness and it encourages my heart. Unfortunately, I feel like I don't see as many of these 'seasoned saints.' It's disappointing because the older should teach the younger. We must value our faith and take the time to develop it, so we can pass this on as an inheritance to 'sons' and 'daughters' that God will send across our path. The next generation needs your faith!

TRUST HIM

Friday

Date: _____

Therefore Sarah laughed within herself, saying, "After I have grown old, shall I have pleasure, my lord being old also?" **-Genesis 18:12-14 (NKJV)**

In the face of God's promise, Sarah laughed. Despite her moment of doubt, Sarah endured the process and obtained the promise! Remember you don't have to know how God will fulfill His promise, just trust Him! Selah

Personal Reflection and Application:

_____
_____
_____
_____
_____
_____
_____
_____
_____
_____

MANIFESTED PROMISES

Saturday

Date: _____

Then the LORD answered me and said: "Write the vision and make it plain on tablets, that he may run who reads it. For the vision is yet for an appointed time; but at the end it will speak, and it will not lie. Though it tarries, wait for it; because it will surely come, it will not tarry. **-Habakkuk 2:2–3 (NKJV)**

It's truly a journey to reach the goals, vision and destiny for your life. I was a little frustrated the other day and received God's encouraging love. He reminded me that on the journey, there will be obstacles—worry, doubt, frustration, naysayers—but it's important to stay focused and keep moving. It will surely come to pass! You shall see the promises of God manifest!

Personal Reflection and Application:

_____
_____
_____
_____
_____
_____
_____
_____
_____
_____
_____

LOVE

Sunday

Date: _____

...to know the love of Christ which passes knowledge; that you may be filled with all the fullness of God. **-Ephesians 3:19 (NKJV)**

How can you "know" something that "passes knowledge"? God's love for you is more than your mind can ever comprehend. You must receive His love by faith. Allow the love of God to saturate your life and receive His fullness!

Personal Reflection and Application:

_____
_____
_____
_____
_____
_____
_____
_____
_____
_____

Weekend 50

Valuable

But we have this treasure in earthen vessels, that the excellence of the power may be of God and not of us. **-2 Corinthians 4: (NKJV)**

God has placed something special in each of us. Sometimes you may not feel valuable but do not allow your feelings to dictate your self-perception. Your worth comes from God and does not change based on the circumstances.

THE GOOD SHEPHERD

Friday

Date: _____

What man of you, having a hundred sheep, if he loses one of them, does not leave the ninety-nine in the wilderness, and go after the one which is lost until he finds it? And when he has found it, he lays it on his shoulders, rejoicing. **-Luke 15:4–5 (NKJV)**

Even in your wilderness experience, know that God has not forgotten about you. Others may seem to be on track and blessed while you are wandering around lost. No worries, the Good Shepherd loves you, and He's coming for you. He's manifesting Himself in your situation. Rejoice! God has not forgotten you!

Personal Reflection and Application:

_____

_____

_____

_____

_____

_____

_____

_____

_____

_____

Capresha Caldwell

COSTLY OIL

Saturday

Date: _____

And behold, a woman in the city who was a sinner, when she knew that *Jesus* sat at the table in the Pharisee's house, brought an alabaster flask of fragrant oil, and stood at His feet behind *Him* weeping; and she began to wash His feet with her tears and wiped *them* with the hair of the head; and she kissed His feet and anointed *them* with the fragrant oil. Now when the Pharisee who had invited Him saw *this*, he spoke to himself, saying, "This Man, if He were a prophet, would know who and what manner of woman *this is* who is touching Him, for she is a sinner." Then He said to her, "Your sins are forgiven. **-Luke 7:37-39, 48 (NKJV)**

Fragrant oil was very expensive and represents something very valuable in life. This woman was thankful to Jesus and she humbled herself. She cried tears of gratitude and anointed His feet. Others may have judged her, but the Lord forgave her. Cece Winans has a song about this scripture and one lyric talks the cost of the oil in her alabaster box. In other words, some people may not know your life's story, but God does. Lay everything before the Lord.

Personal Reflection and Application:

_____
_____
_____
_____
_____
_____
_____
_____
_____
_____

GODLY CONNECTIONS

Sunday

Date: _____

Now at this time Mary arose and hurried to the hill country, to a city of Judah (Judea), and she entered the house of Zacharias and greeted Elizabeth. When Elizabeth heard Mary's greeting, her baby leaped in her womb; and Elizabeth was filled with the Holy Spirit *and* empowered by Him. And she exclaimed loudly, "Blessed [worthy to be praised] are you among women, and blessed is the fruit of your womb! And how has it *happened* to me, that the mother of my Lord would come to me? For behold, when the sound of your greeting reached my ears, the baby in my womb leaped for joy. **-Luke 1:39 – 44 (AMP)**

Despite her age, God blessed Elizabeth with a child. Elizabeth and Mary were pregnant at the same time. Mary was pregnant with baby Jesus, and Elizabeth was pregnant with John the Baptist. When Mary visited Elizabeth, Elizabeth's baby leaped on the inside. They were both pregnant with destiny and God's purpose. You need to connect with women that "makes your baby leap"! Make connections with other women that inspire you to fulfill God's purpose for your life!

Personal Reflection and Application:

_____

_____

_____

_____

_____

_____

_____

_____

_____

_____

_____

206

Weekend 51

For in him we live and move and have our being. **-Acts 17:28a (NKJV)**

When I awoke yesterday, I thought about how I'm still a *child* of God. I love that I will never outgrow my heavenly Father. No matter how old I am, I still rely on God for my life. I admit that some weeks have been a little stressful. It's so important to find an opportunity to find peace and stillness in the presence of God!

PEACE

Friday

Date: _____

[A]nd having strapped on your feet the Gospel of peace in preparation [to face the enemy with firm-footed stability and the readiness produced by the good news]. **-Ephesians 6:15 (AMP)**

[A]nd having shod your feet with the preparation of the gospel of peace; **-Ephesians 6:15 (NKJV)**

Wherever you go, take the peace of God with you! Your presence should change the atmosphere because the Holy Spirit dwells on the inside of you. Speak Words of comfort and encouragement so that others may find rest and peace.

Personal Reflection and Application:

_____

_____

_____

_____

_____

_____

_____

_____

_____

_____

_____

PREPARATION

Saturday

Date: _____

Each young woman's turn came to go into King Ahasuerus and after she had completed twelve months' preparation, according to the regulations for the women, for thus were the days of their preparation apportioned: six months with oil of myrrh, and six months with perfumes and preparations for beautifying women. **-Esther 2:12 (NKJV)**

King Ahasuerus was looking to replace his wife, Queen Vashti, so he called for the young virgins to be presented to him. These ladies had to complete 12 months of preparation before they were brought before the king. For Esther, this was bigger than just getting married - connecting with the King was a part of her destiny. Recognize that you have to go through a time of preparation before you step into the fullness of God's purpose and destiny for your life.

Personal Reflection and Application:

_____
_____
_____
_____
_____
_____
_____
_____
_____
_____
_____

FAVOR

Sunday

Date: _____

Now when the turn came for Esther the daughter of Abihail the uncle of Mordecai, who had taken her as his daughter, to go in to the king, she requested nothing but what Hegai the king's eunuch, the custodian of the women, advised. And Esther obtained favor in the sight of all who saw her. So Esther was taken to King Ahasuerus, into his royal palace, in the tenth month, which *is* the month of Tebeth, in the seventh year of his reign. The king loved Esther more than all of the *other* women, and she obtained grace and favor in his sight more than all the virgins; so he set the royal crown upon her head and made her queen instead of Vashti. - **Esther 2:15 –17 (NKJV)**

When you are fulfilling the purpose of God for your life, He will give you the favor that you need to get into position. He will provide you with the necessary connections. Many times, we are working to get people's attention and approval. Esther didn't do anything extra to get the king's favor. Focus on walking by faith and aligning yourself with God's will for your life.

Personal Reflection and Application:

_____
_____
_____
_____
_____
_____
_____
_____
_____
_____

Weekend 52

Put on the whole armor of God, that you may be able to stand against the wiles of the devil. For we do not wrestle against flesh and blood, but against principalities, against powers, against the rulers of the darkness of this age, against spiritual *hosts* of wickedness in the heavenly *places*. **-Ephesians 6:11 – 12 (NKJV)**

I remember learning about the Armor when I was in college. I would literally stand up and read the scriptures out loud. Like playing an air guitar, I was going through the physical motions of 'putting on my armor.' I would leave my dorm with such a feeling and mindset of empowerment. We have to remember that the battle we are facing is spiritual and not natural. You need spiritual weapons to defeat a spiritual enemy. God has provided the armor to us. We must put it on and stand.

EQUIPPED FOR VICTORY

Friday

Date: _____

Above all, lift up the [protective] shield of faith with which you can extinguish all the flaming arrows of the evil *one*. -**Ephesians 6:16 (AMP)**

I normally wear slacks and a blouse to work. Recently, I switched things up and wore a suit. I felt so powerful and professional. Then I thought about the Armor of God. Putting on the Armor should have a great impact on your confidence – knowing that you are equipped for victory!

Personal Reflection and Application:

_____
_____
_____
_____
_____
_____
_____
_____
_____
_____

Capresha Caldwell

PROTECTED BY FAITH

Saturday

Date: _____

For whatever is born of God overcomes the world. And this is the victory that has overcome the world—our faith. **-1 John 5:4 (NKJV)**

Faith gives us the victory and overcomes the world! Your faith is precious and without it you cannot please God (Hebrews 11:6). Having faith in God protects you! I have a colleague who considers himself to be a 'realist.' In other words, he calls it like he SEES it. I don't ignore the natural circumstances, but I know the situation will improve. When he says it's an impossible situation, I refuse to allow that seed to be planted in my heart. I trust God to open a door and do the impossible! In the store or gas stations, I encounter people that talk about how unaffordable everything is. I don't join in or accept that because by faith I trust God to meet my needs. The Bible says that the enemy is throwing 'flaming arrows' at you – something that will pierce your skin and burn you. Don't get so distracted by a busy life that you fail to lift your shield of faith.

Personal Reflection and Application:

_____
_____
_____
_____
_____
_____
_____
_____
_____
_____
_____

YOU HAVE POWER

Sunday

Date: _____

So David received from her hand what she had brought him, and said to her, "Go up in peace to your house. See, I have heeded your voice and respected your person." **-1 Samuel 25:35 (NKJV)**

Abigail saved a nation! Her husband, Nabal, was a horrific man and was disrespectful to David. When David requested food and water, Nabal refused. In response to his refusal, David set-off with his men to destroy the land. A servant told Abigail about Nabal's inappropriate response. Immediately, Abigail apologized for Nabal's actions and pleaded with David. Because she interceded for her family and the land, everything was spared. Ladies we have to recognize the power that we have to intercede for our family, friends, and our nation!

Personal Reflection and Application:

_____

_____

_____

_____

_____

_____

_____

_____

_____

_____

_____

CPSIA information can be obtained
at www.ICGtesting.com
Printed in the USA
BVHW082043260421
605889BV00016B/571